Analyzing A Common Word Between Us Muslims and You Christians

Analyzing A Common Word Between Us Muslims and You Christians

A Critical Discourse Analysis (CDA)

Joseph Nnabugwu

Library of Congress Control Number:		2011906394
ISBN:	Hardcover	978-1-4628-5306-9
	Softcover	978-1-4628-5305-2
	Ebook	978-1-4628-5307-6

To order additional copies of this book, contact:

Xlibris Corporation
1663 Liberty Drive Suite 200 Bloomington, IN 47403
0-800-644-6988
www.xlibrispublishing.co.uk
Orders@xlibrispublishing.co.uk
301787

Contents

To my late father, Ana-eme Nkpa, Nkpa ana-abia

Acknowledgments

The author would like to thank His Royal Highness Prince Ghazi bin Muhammad, the author of A Common Word and Aftab Ahmed, office director, Royal Islamic Strategic Studies Centre for the permission to use materials:

Appendix A and its uses in extract 1 "An Open Letter and Call from Muslim Religious Leaders to." In *Downloads and Translations A Common Word Between Us and You*, The Official Website of A Common Word, 2007, The Royal Aal al-Bayt Institute for Islamic Thought, Jordan.

Appendix B and its uses in extract 2 "Loving God and Neighbor Together: A Christian Response to *A Common Word between Us and You*." In *A Common Word 'White Paper' Booklet 2008*, The Royal Aal al-Bayt Institute for Islamic Thought, Jordan.

Appendix C and its uses in extract 5 "Final Declaration Issued at the Conclusion of the First Seminar of the Catholic-Muslim Forum, Rome 6 November 2008." In *A Common Word 'White Paper' Booklet 2008*, The Royal Aal al-Bayt Institute for Islamic Thought, Jordan.

Other uses of A Common Word in extracts 3, 4, 6, 7, 8, and 9.

This book is an acknowledgment of the lives of countless men and women, each of whom has helped enhance the manners Muslims and Christians come together.

Introduction

The purpose of this book is to analyze a common word,[1] its source and reason for its invention, and to use critical discourse analysis (CDA) as an approach in the analysis of extracts of *A Common Word 'White Paper' Booklet 2008*.[2] A common word is not only a peace initiative derived from the Qur'anic *surah Al-'Imran 3:64*; it is also an assemblage of communiqués, declarations, and outcomes of seminars, workshops, fora, letters, and speeches from Islamic religious leaders and scholars and Christian religious leaders and scholars that become major parts that form a common word White Paper.

What Is A Common Word?

Qur'anically, the phrase *a common word* is derived from *surah Al-'Imran 3:64*: "Say: O People of the Scripture! Come to a common word between us and you: that we shall worship none but God, and that we shall ascribe no partner unto Him, and that none of us shall take others for lords beside God." There is the claim that the People of the Book (that is, the term used to refer to Jews, Christians, and Sabians because they possess the Torah, the *Injil* [Gospel], and the Psalms) agree to all three propositions of a common word—"that we shall worship none but God" and "that we shall ascribe no partner unto Him" and "that none of us shall take others for lords beside

God"; however, in reality, they all fail (Yusuf 'Ali 2008, p. 144). It appears that Abdullah Yusuf 'Ali reckons the doctrinal disparity in the unity of God. Between Christianity and Islam, the former's emphasis is the Blessed Trinity that is there are three persons in one God: God the Father, God the Son, and God the Holy Spirit), while the latter's emphasis is Tawhid (that is there is no god but God; it suggests the uniqueness and oneness of God). Islam questions at the same time the consecrated priesthood in Christianity and the veneration of saints. It can be said that a common word is a Qur'anic invitation to its concept of God as against every other.

It could be argued that a common word call mainly highlights the Islamic monotheism known as Tawhid and invites the People of the Book to embrace Islamic definition of monotheism. The label "a common word between us and you" (Al-'Imran 3:64) and its concept raise the issues of difference between us Muslims and you Christians or the other People of the Book and call for a representation of a particular concept of monotheism—Tawhid. This forms the departure of a common word project. It, however, attracted a rival and, to some extent, corresponding responses from Christian church hierarchies and religious leaders and scholars. Several responses from Muslim scholars and religious leaders, Christian scholars and religious leaders, communiqués, declarations, and outcomes of seminars and workshops, fora, letters, and speeches become major parts of the White Paper. Gradually, a common word has become a peace initiative between Muslims and Christians. As presented in the official website (see OWACW 2007), a common word is an amalgam of first-congregational-styled presentations of Muslims and Christians' discourses; its White Paper becomes an official report based on agreement of both Muslim and Christian religious leaders/scholars on policies that will form the basis of their relationships. These agreements were published on the official website of a common word and maintained by the Royal Aal al-Bayt Institute for Islamic Thought, Jordan (see OWACW 2007).

It is a qualitative discourse that was developed by and for Muslim-Christian interfaith dialogue that underlines the discourses of the ideologies based on the different religious communities' definition of *monotheism*. Using the framework of CDA, a common word is analyzed as a qualitative data by exposing the underlying problems of ideologies, dichotomies, identity constructions, and orthodoxies that are associated with the claims of both Muslims and Christians in regard to the unity of God. In its application of CDA approach, this book contests some assumptions like Tony Blair's (quoted in Volf et al. 2010) that "the language or concept of love itself is" capable "of addressing the truly thorny and important issues that challenge Muslim-Christian coexistence and cooperation." One of the reasons of CDA application is to clarify such "soft and nebulous emotion" like Blair's that misses the point. Though religious leaders/scholars of both Islam and Christianity construct their ideological positions and identities from their different understanding of their concepts of monotheism, there is the observation that groups of Muslims and Christians, through various conferences and workshops, were able to reach some compromises on interfaith matters.

As this book is aimed at examining and analyzing a common word discourse, it primarily asks the following: How would discourse analysis help in the attempt to authentic communication in Muslim-Christian relations? How have the Muslims and Christians discursively constructed themselves, especially from the discourses of religious leaders/scholars? These questions are answered when it applies the framework of CDA to a common word White Paper in order to further expose the ideologies associated with the Tawhid and Trinity in terms of identity constructions, *valuing* and *representing* in the discourses of both Muslim and Christian religious leaders/scholars. The reason is that in the use of CDA framework, efforts will be made to examine the texts and analyze how the claims to orthodoxy are produced and reproduced and the ways identity construction based on the concepts of God have continued to dichotomize the relations between Islam and Christianity.

The application of the framework of CDA to the analysis of a common word articulates among other things by discourse-historical, social psychology, and linguistics approaches the fluid relationship between Muslims and Christians and the problems associated with a common word. The White Paper of a common word asserts within the "Frequently Asked Questions" (FAQ) section that the mechanics of its production started with the *"Amman Message and its interfaith components.* Then the idea was mentioned in summary in the October 2006 'Open Letter to the Pope'" (see ACWWP 2008). Pope Benedict XVI could be said to have influenced the urgency for the need for the White Paper. This is because it was alleged that he offended the Muslim world in his thought-provoking "Address at the University of Regensburg, Germany, September 12, 2006." In this address, he quoted a medieval Byzantine emperor, Manuel II, who was arguing with a Persian interlocutor on the relationship between religion and violence: "Show me just what Mohammad brought that was new, and there you will find things only evil and inhuman, such as his command to spread by the sword the faith he preached."[3] The Papal Address generated a lot of condemnation from the Muslim world, both from religious leaders and scholars as well as youths. This necessitated several conferences and gatherings of Muslims that reached climax in their last meeting that was on "Love in the Qur'an." The product of it was a final draft to a common word that was followed by some additional signatories (from 38 to 138 to 460) to authenticate the document.

The representatives in the signatories as claimed by the White Paper were profiled and consultative of Muslim "religious authorities, scholars, intellectuals, media experts, professionals" (see ACWWP 2008). Besides, various schools of mainstream Islam were also in consultation: "*Sunni* (from *Salafis* to *Sufis*), *Shi'i* (*Ja'fari, Ziadi, Ishma'ili*), and *Ibadi.*" It is noted that the author of the document is His Royal Highness (HRH) Prince Ghazi bin

Muhammad. Not only was the document authenticated by the signatories, it has also been checked and approved by a group of senior Ulema including Sheikh Ali Goma, (grand mufti of Egypt), Sheikh Abd Allah bin Bayyah, (an Islamic jurist raised in Mauritania who has a lot of students considered as Ulemas in their own rights), and Sheikh Sa'id Ramadan al-Buti, (a scholar who presently holds membership in the Royal Society of the Islamic Civilization Researches in Amman, Jordan) (see ACWWP 2008).

The White Paper argues that the world is in turmoil. Therefore, peace between Islam and Christianity is an important and a necessary condition to world peace; it claims that the adherents of these two religions combined make up more than half of the population of the world. In response, Christian religious leaders and scholars were stimulated by its content. It started with some individual Christian religious leaders/scholars to a group response of over three hundred, leading Christian scholars to "a common word between us and you."

The structure of this book consists of seven chapters. Chapter 1 deals with the appositional pronouns *us* and *you* and views them as points of references in the review of the universe of discourses on the kinds of relationships that exist between Muslims and Christians. Chapter 2 evaluates the CDA approaches, methods, frameworks, criticisms, and the whys of a common word as data for investigation. Chapter 3 analyzes a common word following Norman Fairclough's framework (2001): "Stage 1: Locating the Social Problems in the Research Question (or Primary Questions)" and "Stage 2: Identifying the Problems to Be Tackled." Besides, it makes an interactional analysis of the White Paper. Chapter 4 deals with the Open Letter and Call. Based on Fairclough's analytical framework, this book makes a summary of extract 1 in the form of interactional analysis; it continues with the interdiscursive analysis, linguistic analysis (examining the whole-text organization), clause combination, clauses, and words. Chapter 5 is the Christian response to the Muslim religious leaders' Open Letter and Call, a discourse by which the semiotic is influenced. Analyzing extract 2 and in like manner of extract 1, it applies Fairclough's framework: interactional analysis, interdiscursive analysis, linguistic analysis (examining the whole-text organization), clause combination, clauses, and words. A common word project is viewed as Muslim-Christian conscious efforts and move to authentic communication in chapter 6. It is an interfaith initiative rising up to a "meeting-point-ness" of Muslims and Christians. Finally, inasmuch as some groups of Muslim and Christian religious leaders and scholars came to some resolutions, delivered communiqués and final statements and declarations, the analyses from stages 1-4 of the entire exercise showed that the people on the grassroots level are in marginality in the entire order of discourses. A common word was structured to be a communication between Muslims and Christians constructed from "above" (religious leaders and scholars of both religions) and did not involve directly those from "below" (that is, from the grassroots).

Chapter One

Us Muslims and You Christians

These appositional pronouns *us* and *you* are considered as points of references in the review of the universe of discourses on the kinds of relationships that exist between Muslims and Christians. The adjective *appositional* is used here in the sense of placing *us* and *you* side by side. When viewed from the perspective of full citation of Qur'anic *Al-'Imran* 3:64, it evokes some emotional suspicion of substitutiveness or subtractiveness. It is argued here that excessive use of *us* and *you* in a sense is a flirtation with particularist religionist construct. Following the Qur'anic command to a common word between *us* and *you* (*Al-'Imran* 3:64) are the numerous propositions and arguments concerning the relationships, progresses, understandings, and dialogues between Muslims and Christians. Therefore, it is proper to underscore the prospects of consolidating the relationships and managing and containing the differences between Muslims and Christians. It is necessary also to make a review of the dimensionality of this relationship by way of pronominal category, which is examining *us* and *you* as pronouns in English grammar and their power to influence. Among scholars, claims regarding the relationship between Muslims and Christians vary. The variations start from the frameworks suggesting brotherhood or sisterhood in the frames of *Ummah* consciousness or ecumenism (Abedin 1990, Cragg 1999, Hick 2000), the pluralist religious strategy (Hick 1989, 1997, 2000; Panikkar 1999; Heim 1995; Knitter 1987, 1995) to the perspectives of evaluation of dialogues based on similarities and differences on their belief systems.

The courage of Seyyed Nasr is admired here when he carefully chose a phrase *we and you*, which is a Qur'anic initiative as part of the title of his address "We and You—Let us Meet in God's Love" presented at the papal audience at the "First Seminar of the Catholic-Muslim Forum Rome," 2008. Nasr (2008) was repeatedly and simultaneously dialoguing with both Muslims and Christians at a time: "*We* and *you* are both members of the family of Abrahamic monotheism." Nasr could be said to have fallen for a universalist theological understanding of the Real (Hick 1989). Muslims and Christians are near match in many belief systems and practices: "For both *us* and *you*, God is at once transcendent and immanent . . . *We* and *you* both revere Christ but in a different manner . . . *You* and *we*, we both believe in religious freedom" and "the border of the definition of neighbor to include not only *you* and *us* but the whole of humanity" (Nasr 2008). The key point of this "universalist phenomenalist pluralism" (McGarvey 2009) is a faithful recognition of the *Al-'Imran* 3:64 mandate. But is it what Nasr meant? Though *us* and *you* have dialogue at its basis, they suggest in one sense that both Muslims and Christians are close in kinship as Abrahamic religions. But in another sense, they suggest a wide gap of difference between us Muslims and you Christians. Drawing from English language, the pronominal category of *us* and *you* is examined below in the context of us Muslims and you Christians. This is based on their grammatical implication and how they can be used to differentiate entities.

Pronominal Category

Pronoun in English grammar is one of a class of words that is introduced to replace a noun or noun phrase mentioned already or about to be mentioned in the context. In the context of this book, the pronouns involved directly are observed in this Qur'anic citation "Say: O People of the Book! Come to common word between us and you: that we worship none but Allah; that we associate no partners with Him; that we erect not, from among ourselves, Lords and patrons other than Allah" (*Al-'Imran* 3:64). The most important pronouns for this exercise are *us* and *you*. According to Randolph Quirk, Sidney Greenbaum, Geoffrey Leech, and Jan Svartvik (1985, p. 335), pronouns are best seen "as comprising a varied class of closed-class words with nominal function. By 'nominal' here we mean 'noun-like' or more frequently, 'like a noun phrase'"; and for them, pronouns may either "substitute for some word or phrase ... signal as personal pronouns" or "stand for a very general concept." This book considers the appositional pronouns *us* and *you* in the context of *Al-'Imran* 3:64, as general concepts denoting us Muslims and you Christians or other People of the Book.

The three distinctions of persons in pronouns will help give further understanding to this pronominal category of the contextual *us* and *you*. The distinctions include the following:

> First Person Pronouns—I, me, my, mine, myself, we, us, our, ours, ourselves
> Second Person Pronouns—you, your, yours, yourself, yourselves
> Third Person Pronouns—he, him, his, himself, she, her, hers, herself, it, its, itself, they, them, their, theirs, themselves.

The first person pronouns refer to the speaker(s) or writer(s), the producer(s) or reproducer(s) of the message; the second person pronouns refer to the addressee(s) or reader(s), the audience or the recipient(s), and the third person pronouns refer to third parties—that is, both the persons involved in the first person and the second person pronouns. The argument here with regard to the appositional pronouns *us* and *you* is that if pronouns have coordinated antecedents, "the choice of pronoun is determined by ... an order of precedence whereby the first person outweighs the second person" (Quirk et al. 1985, p. 355). In the context of this analysis, *us* here has precedence over *you*; *us* also outweighs *you*.

The appositional pronouns *us Muslims* and *you Christians* reveal some ideological flavor. The Qur'anic *surah Al-'Imran* 3:64 cited above presents series of nonrestrictive clauses. For some grammarians, "non-restrictive clauses are parenthetic comments which usually describe ... the antecedent" (Quirk et al. 1985, p. 366). In this context, *us* and *you* are antecedents presented as parallels in equality in terms of monotheistic beliefs; however, judging from the prescriptive clauses of *Al-'Imran* 3:64 (that we worship none but Allah, that we associate no partners with Him, that we erect not, from among ourselves, Lords and patrons other than Allah), there is suggestion of variations in terms of functional relationship between Muslims and Christians. It might be said that *you* are invited to a pact of truth that suggests a revision or change of their belief system. Michael Swan (2009, p. 67) opined that the problem with prescriptive rules is that they "impose beliefs of the people who devised them; they convey opinions, not facts." Can that be said of the functional relationship between *us Muslims* and *you Christians?*

From another angle, the use of a type of conjunctive cohesion *and* within the domain of extension or expansion (see Halliday 1985, pp. 302-309) suggests that us Muslims *and* you Christians or other People of the Book are included in the true course of monotheism. It suggests an equal and interdependent monotheistic belief terms. In a way, *and* here suggests a type of conjunction that expresses "the semantic relationship between the units they connect, reflecting the speaker's view of the connection between states of affairs in the world" (Downing and Locke 2006, p. 294). The plural pronouns of all persons, like in *us* and *you*, can function generically with reference to "people in general" (Quirk et al. 1985, p. 353); but *us* and *you* as used in Qur'anic *surah Al-'Imran* 3:64 suggests the strictest meaning, the meaning that refers to Muslims as *us* and the People of the Book as *you*. Moreover, if *we* is to be used in place of *us* and *you*, it could be argued then that *we* is used in the context of "rhetorical *we*"; that is, it is used in the collective sense of "the People of the Book" or "the whole world" (see Quirk et al. 1985, p. 350). Nevertheless, in this book, the use of *us* and *you* refers to the relationship between Muslims and Christians; by way of analysis, the relationship could extend to non-Muslims.

Ummah Consciousness

Us and *you* could mean that Muslims and Christians are in brotherhood or sisterhood, but it can also mean a brotherhood or sisterhood defined exclusively by the individual religious community's spirit, or it can mean Muslims and the rest of the world. The Qur'an, for example, has a popular cryptonym *Ummah*, which calls Muslims to come together as brothers and sisters especially in a non-Muslim jurisdiction. Syed Abedin (1990, pp. 2-3) defines such Muslims as being in minority, and for him a minority Muslim is

> one who lives under non-Muslim Jurisdiction, in a society where Islam is not the prevailing religion or culture, where there are no positive incentives to the growth and nurture of Islamic values and norms and where even under the best of circumstances, a deliberate and persistent effort has to be made to preserve Islamic identity.

Such community spirit identified by brotherhood or sisterhood is an invocation of the *Ummah consciousness*: "The believers, men and women, are protectors of one another: they enjoin what is just, and forbid what is evil" (*Al-Tawbah* 9:71). Again the Qur'an reiterates this call further: "The believers are but a single brotherhood: so make peace and reconciliation between your two (contending) brothers; and fear Allah, that ye may receive mercy" (*Al-Hujurat* 49:10). Abedin (1990, p. 6) claims that

> here, we start with the assumption that the concept of the ummah in Islam involves a "consciousness of community"; that Muslims, once Muslims, develop a "sense of belongingness" with other believers in the same faith. We also assume on the basis of contemporary evidence that this "sense of belongingness" is still to be among today's myriads and manifold Muslims.

The consciousness of community stratagem could not only be viewed as an orthodox position; it is also a *consciousness* that calls one Muslim group (the Muslim-majority countries) to meet the Islamic obligations of *Ummah* consciousness in another group (the Muslim-minority communities) (Abedin 1990).

Christian Ecumenism

The Christians themselves are obsessed by the commonweal of brotherhood and sisterhood, which at times is summarized in the concept of ecumenism (call of unity among all Christian churches). In more general terms, Kenneth Cragg (1999) advocated for religious prevalence from the perspectives of universalism and humanism. In an interview framed "Cross Meets Crescent," he tried to give his understanding of ecumenism from the Muslim perspective. When asked what ecumenism looks like from a Muslim perspective, in response, he etymologized the word *ecumenism*: "The word *ecumenae* means the whole inhabited world. But we seem to have limited it to Christian togetherness, to Christian mutuality. Couldn't we have an *ecumenae* of religions?" He tended to make a swap of both terms *Christian* and *religion*. According to him, the ecumenical movement has adopted the position that "whatever is Christian I will try to belong with, in some sense. Can we go on to say, I will try to belong with anything that is religious?" This can be a difficult and unrealizable dream. Because religion is not only a subculture of the "whole inhabited world," there are other predications like secularism and atheism that also form part of the "whole inhabited world."

In addition to the above, John Hick (2000, p. 2) argues that the word *ecumenism* belongs to every religion. He suggests that "the ecumenical developments needed within each faith community have to be brought about from within that faith community. The only way in which one tradition can usefully influence another in its direction is by example." The foregoing arguments presuppose that the concept of religion can be universalized from different perspectives; however, communal religion could be viewed as an individual and community's practices of spirituality. Cragg (1999) expressed some fears that "religion is such an omnibus term . . . Would we want to align ourselves with the Hinduism that undergirds the caste system or the Hinduism of Gandhi, which repudiates the caste system? To which Islam can Christians relate—the Islam of Afghanistan's Taliban or the Islam of academics living in the West?" Similarly, the Muslims could be in the dilemma about Christianity. Do they relate with the Christianity of Trinitarianism or the Christianity of Unitarianism? Cragg did not point out this. But he affirms that "with due circumspection, I think it's possible to relate to those of other faiths. If we agree to agree, we must at the same time agree to disagree. Otherwise, we may be heading only for some kind of gooey sentimentalism."

Thinking about Christian-Muslim relations as a correlation of implicit and explicit attitudes, Rowatt et al. (2005, p. 29) carried out their investigation in an environment that was predominantly Christian in the United States. Technically, they assessed the implicit attitudes with what is known as Implicit Association Test (IAT), a computer program that recorded reaction times as participants categorized names (of Christians and Muslims) and adjectives (pleasant or unpleasant). They observed that Christians' implicit and explicit evaluations of the in-group (i.e., Christians) are more favorable than their implicit and explicit evaluations of the out-group (i.e., Muslims). Basing their pattern of study with social identity theory (Tajfel 1982), they recommend that "on the interpersonal level, broadening social identity might reduce pervasive in-group/out-group biases."

Besides, it might be argued that if the same IAT is carried out in a predominantly Muslim environment, the result might be as close as the above. The Muslims' implicit and explicit evaluations of the in-group (i.e., Muslims) could be more favorable than their implicit and explicit evaluations of the out-group (i.e., Christians). In essence, the Christians are more comfortable with fellow Christians than with the Muslims in a predominantly Christian environment; in a similar manner, the Muslims would be more comfortable with fellow Muslims than with the Christians in a predominantly Muslim environment. Nevertheless, Muslims and Christians can be said to be so near that they can now hold some conversations. They are near in matters of religious sophistication, geographical proximity, civilization discourse, and almost attaining equality in numerical strength. These kinds of interrelations can, as Stanislaw Grodz (2007, p. 207) argued, help Muslims and Christians "cast away prejudices and clarifies their perception of others." To uphold the theology of pluralism, suggests Grodz (2007, p. 206), is to be involved in a dialogical way of doing mission. Taking inspiration from the Qur'anic *Al-Ma'ida* 5:48, Grodz (2007, p. 207) insists that "'vying in good works' also means striving for spiritual development in a way that does not apply any pressure on others to accept someone else's point of view and convictions."

Pluralist Religious Strategy

At times, inasmuch as people agree to agree or disagree to agree, Zein (2003, p. 23) noted that the richness in thought and diversity, rather than uniformity, is shown to be intentional in the divine scheme. According to him, the search for uniformity envisaged by some mentalities entails "heresy" by necessity. Whereas, vying between ethnic and religious communities should be in good deeds only, not in enmity or mutual hostility. Complete uniformity is never envisaged by the Qur'an. The Qur'an itself isn't speaking about originality, rather humans are. Furthermore, the Qur'an makes it categorically clear without exempting any peoples that "those who believe (in the Qur'an), and those who follow the Jewish (scriptures), and the Christians and the Sabians—any who believe in Allah and the Last Day, and work righteousness, shall have their reward with their Lord; on them shall be no fear, nor shall they grieve" (Al-Baqarah 2:62).

Among some theologians and philosophers of religion, the perspectives of exclusivism, inclusivism, and pluralism stand out (Zebiri 1997, Platinga 1998). Exclusivists adopt positions that deny the possibility of truth claims to other religions. They consider their truth claims as absolute, incontrovertible, and inaccessible from without (Crafford 1995, Westerlund 2003, Panikkar 2000). The inclusivists make some truth claims for their religions but at the same time accept the fact that other religions have access to the same truth claims (Panikkar 2000). Raymond Panikkar (1999) conceived the mystery or transcendent as beyond one Real. For him, therefore, religions should be better understood through the mystical experience of the Real and not doctrinally. This new way of interreligious understanding seeks relationship and harmony.

Hick (2000, p. 5) views the concept of religion from pluralistic standpoint: "In terms of truth claims, exclusivism holds that Christianity alone has the final Truth; inclusivism holds that while this is so, there are lesser truths within other religions; and pluralism holds that each faith has its own truths about its own manifestation of the Ultimate, with each belief-system being integral to a genuine context of salvation." The above acknowledges the fact that pluralism might be one of the ways of containing or managing "the absolutism of the world religions, and particularly of the great monotheisms . . . For the Absolute Truth takes precedence over everything else and can justify anything to defend or assert it" (Hick 2000, p. 1). In this context, pluralism summons the courage of conscientious and dialogic relations. Hick's universalist theology of religions considers all religions as having one common point of religious attention, the Real, and one purpose of belief, salvation. Thus, in interfaith dialogues, different religious communities can learn to admire and explore the riches in different understandings of the ultimate reality (Hick 1989).

Mark Heim (1995), with his particularist theology of religions, argued for the possibility of various religious fulfillments or salvations. But these salvations or religious fulfillments are experienced differently. Basing his pluralism on liberating justice, Paul Knitter (1987, 1995) argues that when people are pulled together because of their common grounds or concerns, there is the tendency for them to form friendships and trust. And this action and total commitment could become better means of doctrinal clarification and understanding (Knitter 2002). Knitter's argument is a score with a common word project. The *us* and *you* between Muslims and Christians for centuries have been one of rivalries, negativities, suspicions, violent conflicts, and polemics. It is not part of this book to discuss early contacts between Islam and Christianity or the Crusades.

Dialogue

By way of historical investigation, Michael FitzGerald embarked on a thirty-year survey of the recent developments between Muslims and Christians. He was very particular with the catholic faith as dialoguing with Islam, especially as the Second Vatican Council, through its declaration *Nostra Aetate* (n. 3), states that the church has "a high regard for Muslims." FitzGerald (2000) remarked that at different periods and in different places, the relationship has been that of cooperation observing the Christian contributions to the Islamic assimilation of the Greek heritage in Abbasid times, the cultural developments in Ummayad Spain and in Sicily under the Normans, the collaboration of Christians and Muslims during the *Nahda*, and the Arab renaissance. However, some highlights of some factors that tended to stifle the relations were noted: "The Islamic world and the Western Christian world became two blocs, a division which the Crusades helped to perpetuate . . . then the colonial era which brought about a 'love-hate relationship' with the Christian West" (FitzGerald 2000, FitzGerald and Borelli 2006). Nevertheless, the Catholic Church pledges to the definitions of *Nostra Aetate* (n. 3) through her curia. According to one Catholic prelate named Francis Cardinal Arinze in his speech to the Centre for Muslim-Christian Understanding, Georgetown University, Washington, DC, in 1997, "a planned study of the other religion is required if interreligious relationships are not to stagnate at the superficial level of generalizations and clichés." He was of the view that "authentic dialogue demands that Muslims and Christians accept one another with all their similarities and differences in matters theological, moral and cultural."

In many ways, religion can be a diplomatic means to peace dialogue. Muhammad Iqbal conceives religion as an invitation to interfaith dialogue. In interpreting Iqbal's conception of religion, it is relevant to examine David Kerr's own analysis of "Muhammad Iqbal's Thoughts on Religion: Reflections in the Spirit of Christian-Muslim Dialogue." That doesn't mean that whatever Kerr says is taken as the whole truth and, as such, that his conclusions should be adopted. Rather, this book considers his framework as a reflection in the spirit of Muslim-Christian dialogue to be nurtured and promoted. He vouchsafed to his neutrality,

> Of one thing I am sure, however. My faith is not in a presumed "Christian" God, distinct from a presumed "Muslim" God. The very thought is idolatrous, and is utterly alien to the theology of Iqbal. His reflections upon God transcend the doctrinal straight-jackets of any religious system, and though he is always loyal to the orthodoxy of Islam, he expresses his thoughts in a manner which

invites the harmonious interaction of believers of other religious traditions. (Kerr 1989, p. 34)

Having said that, Kerr (1989, p. 36), in his intellectual multiculturalism, maintains that Iqbal felt the sensitivity of Christian theology but apparently rejected the Christian notions of incarnation and Trinity: "The reality of God's being is beyond the imperfection of multiplicity, and as the Perfect Individual God's Names, which we construe as many, exist in eternal Unicity." Say, God is One (*ahad*); all things depend on Him (*al-samad*)."" Iqbal further expressed the uniqueness of God by adopting the Qur'anic verses of *surat al-tawhid*: "He begetteth not, and He is not begotten; and there is none like unto Him" (Al-Ikhlas 112). Kerr (1989, p. 37) emphasized that Iqbal was conscious that some polemicists or apologists may misuse the verse to attack Christian theology. He claimed that Iqbal's "argument is essentially against pantheism which he sees as a tendency in all religions to escape from 'an individualistic conception of the Ultimate Reality' and to conceive of God rather as 'a vague, vast and pervasive cosmic element.'" Iqbal's argument is against pantheism, and Christian theology never approves of pantheism but the Trinity and the incarnation. The trouble remains: How would the latter Christian's doctrines be reconciled with the Qur'anic doctrine of Tawhid?

To take this argument further, the 2008 World Economic Forum report titled *Islam and the West: Annual Report on the State of Dialogue*, brings to the fore the problematic of comparing Islam and the West. In other words, the title of the above-mentioned forum could be viewed as *us* (Muslims) and *you* (West). This report presents Islam (a religion) as dialoguing with a particular region (the West). Among other things, the report claims in its definition of the West and Islam the following:

In this report, the "West" refers mainly to Europe and lands of significant European settlement, primarily North America, but also Australia and New Zealand. The definition is geographical-historical rather than cultural. Today, Christianity, Judaism, liberal democracy, free markets, individualism and consumer culture, while part of a European legacy, are increasingly transnational and global phenomena . . . The term "Islam," in this report refers to a religion that finds diverse cultural expression around the world. There is no single overarching "Islamic civilization." (Rienstra and Tranchet 2008)

It could be argued as well that Islam is both a transnational and global phenomenon because of its cultural expression *to* the world, especially in non-Muslim nations. It is a matter of fact statement of Islamic expansion and globalizing. However, it could be argued as well that some Muslim scholars or leaders do adopt civilization discourse in order to stereotype the West as colonialist and imperialist (Ibrahim 2008). Samuel Huntington's *The Clash of Civilizations and the Remaking of World Order* (2002) argues that to identify Christianity to the West as belonging to it is no longer valid; this argument is very nebulous to the claim that Christianity is not the problem of Muslims in the West. According to Hans Kochler (1999, pp. 97-107), "in the context of the political-military confrontations religion served as an ideological tool on the part of Christianity to defend the interests of European rulers—including the head of the Holy See in Rome." Ideologically, Christian values still influence the actions of western political thoughts.

Some Islamic scholars might argue that, "Islam and the West" construct is derivative from the Christian missionaries' apologetics on researches about Islam and Prophet Muhammad. Addressing the misrepresentation and misrecognition of Prophet Muhammad in Western scholarship, Jabal Buaben (1996) moved from the medieval polemical works, typically the influential English writers—William Muir, David S. Margoliouth, and William M. Watt—to twentieth-century works, appraising at the same time the "ideological squares"—us and them—between Islam and the West. Accordingly, Richardson (2007, p. 51) noted that Teun van Dijk developed a conceptual tool that he called the ideological square, which is characterized by a *positive self-presentation* and a simultaneous *negative other-presentation*:

> The ideological square predicts that "outsiders" of various types will be represented in a negative way and "insiders" will be represented in a positive way. This occurs by emphasising (what is called foregrounding) "their" negative characteristics and social activities and de-emphasising (or backgrounding) "their" positive characteristics and social activities . . . This ideological square is observable across all linguistic dimensions of a text. Starting with referential strategies, positive terms are used to refer to "Us" and "Our country" and negative words being used to refer to "Them," "Their country," "Their values."

Anwar Ibrahim's "Islam and the West: The Myth of the Great Dichotomy" (2008, p. 58) viewed Western conception of Muslim as an inherited "baggage of history." He argues that the description of the Muslim "other" "from Mark Twain to Francis Fukuyama and Samuel Huntington has been a matter of academic intrigue as well as popular disdain, often bordering on outright racism," and he links this further to "the cartoon controversy, Pope Benedict's opinion on the Prophet of Islam and the apparent exclusionary stance adopted by many in Western Europe on Turkey's accession to the EU." Edward Said's *Orientalism* (1979) is a reprise of earlier Christian apologetics that placed Christianity as superior and orthodox religion while Islam was taken as a heresy. It is proper to note here that to seek dialogue between Islam and the West only and to background the cultural effects of Christianity is to denigrate the substantial basis of forming relationship. Kochler (1999) argues that to understand the metaphysical concepts in Islam and Christianity is sine qua non in understanding the role they play in shaping the relations between both communities in Europe.

Various scholars have given their opinions about dialogue to resonate around faith traditions even if it is the case of Islam and the West. Karen Armstrong (2008) suggested three areas for encounters between the various traditions: (1) ready to listen to the other, (2) dialoguing not to win, (3) dialoguing not only with like-minded people but to include people of all age-group. Lolowah Alfaisal's "The State of West-Islamic Dialogue" (2008) sees the "Islam and the West" dialogue as a subterfuge to overcome "the conceptual and methodological problems that plague discussions of Islam and the West." For example, she argues that the problems of who represents Islam, Judaism, and Christianity and finding a neutral language for "interreligious and intercultural understanding" are dialogical bottlenecks. Peter Berger would refer to such subterfuge (West-Islamic) as a "categorical mistake." John Esposito's "A Dialogue for Results" (2008) argues that "phrases such as 'Muslim world and the West,' 'West-Islamic, like their counterpart'—'clash of civilizations'—as category mistakes fail to adequately reflect a complex, multifaceted reality" that includes the political, economic, and religious. Esposito (2008, p. 18) acknowledges that "ironically, in a world of globalization when pluralism and tolerance have never been more important, hegemonic and exclusivist ideologies and theologies are ascendant." Dialogue at times is viewed as a mask to perpetuate oppression. Mozah Al-Missned's "West-Islamic Dialogue: What It Is Really About" introduces Franz Fanon to unmask the obscuring language in the dialogue between Islam and the West. She argues that the West dialogue campaign with Russia, China, and Japan is very different from their dialogue campaign in the Middle East. She claims that

> the Middle East is a much less powerful adversary, much less capable
> of gaining the upper hand in technological battles or propaganda
> wars. Therefore, the struggles for power across the region are almost

always referred to in terms that obscure the unequal balance of power—as an ideological and eternal cultural and religious conflict. (2008, p. 35)

Jane McAuliffe (2008) would argue that real, productive and deep dialogue take time and trust. Hence, she claims that there is a need to step out from behind the precast characters of orthodoxy claims of Christianity and Islam respectively. Daniel Sachs (2008) argues for a larger integration of all people, especially those in minority in Europe, into the fabric of European society. While Maria van der Hoeven (2008) sees dialogue from the perspective of respect of the "other." The prospect of dialogue of Mustafa Ceric (2008) embodies using the past to build the future. The above exposition expands the horizon of the phrase *us and you.*

Chapter Two

—※—

Method to A Common Word

To investigate on the primary question of how discourse analysis can help in authentic communication in Muslim-Christian relations, it is pertinent here to analyze the methodology adopted in the analysis of the texts extracts of the White Paper (see appendices A and B). It is argued here for an understanding of discourse analysis because it will help in the understanding of CDA. The intention in this book is to use Norman Fairclough's CDA framework; therefore, its fundamental will be particularly analyzed and applied. There are varieties of theories leading to the concept of discourse analysis. Discourse analysis is a very contested concept whose definition goes beyond the scope of discourse studies itself (Richardson 2007, p. 21). This makes "discourse" to have different interpretations. Discourse analysis could be viewed as the "study of talk and text" and "as a set of methods and theories for investigating language in use and language in social context" (Wetherell et al. 2001, i). As such, "language," according to Margaret Wetherell and Jonathan Potter (1987, p. 9), "is so central to all social activities." Richardson (2007, p. 10) also considers language as "social" and central to human activity. Discourse analysis can be said to be a language-oriented program. Discourse then is seen as a way of handling language. By way of definition, inasmuch as definitions seem to place ceilings on concepts, Jonathan Potter (1997, p. 146) defined discourse analysis as

> an analytic commitment to studying discourse as texts and talk in social practices. That is, the focus is not on language as an abstract entity such as a lexicon and set of grammatical rules (in linguistics), a system of differences (in structuralism), a set of rules for transforming statements (in Foucauldian genealogies). Instead, it is the medium for interaction; analysis of discourse becomes, then, analysis of what people do.

Furthermore, Schiffrin (1994) and Richardson (2007, p. 22) argue that there are two general approaches to discourse analysis: the *formalist* or *structuralist* definition of discourse and the *functionalist* definition of discourse. The *formalist* definition of discourse as "language above the sentence" makes discourse and the "theorists who adopt this first definition of discourse tend to look at the features which link sentences together; the formal features which make two sentences 'a discourse' rather than just two unconnected phrases." Language, as noted above, involves also social activities, and because of this very fact, the *formalist* definition of discourse analysis is not enough. Wetherell et al. (2001) and Taylor (2001) describe discourse analysis as the close study of "language in use." The phrase *language in use* brings out the social aspect of discourse. The understanding of language as social is reflected in the second broad definition of *discourse*, that is, the *functionalist* definition (Brown and Yule 1983, Richardson 2007). *Functionalists* think that language is active and discourse analysis is the examination and investigation of what people do with language (Cameron 2001, Richardson 2007).

There is a claim here that both *formalist* and *functionalist* applications of "language use" and "language in use" are to be adopted when analyzing a common word White Paper. The idea of "common representational system" (Wetherell and Potter 1987) makes language a sine qua non in social activities. Some scholars argue that discourse analysis is a perspective on social life that contains both methodological and conceptual elements that comprise also ways of thinking about discourse (theoretical and metatheoretical elements) and ways of treating discourse as data (methodological elements) (Kroger and Wood 2000). The "theoretical" and "metatheoretical" have developed into multiple perspectives of discourse analysis as defining methodologies of qualitative study. The conceptualizations of discourse have meaning because of this connectivity.

Theoretically and methodologically, discourse analysis has made roads in social psychology and feminism (Burman and Parker 1993, Potter and Wetherell 2004, van Dijk 1983); in social relations of power, domination, and ideology (Chouliaraki and Fairclough 2004; Fairclough 1995, 2001; Fairclough and Wodak 1997; Habermas 1971; Forgacs 1988; Althusser 1971; Bakhtin 1986; Foucault 2000); in ethnomethodology (Garfinkel 1967); in linguistic and conversational analyses (Atkinson and Drew 1979; Sacks 1992; Schegloff 1972, 1992; ten Have 1999); in social constructionism (Burr 2003, Gergen 1996); in semiotic (Wetherell et al. 2001; Fairclough 2001; Chandler 1994; Derrida 1976; Saussure 1974, 1983; Pierce 1931-58). The above gives the impression that scholars in the application of discourse analysis have employed different analytic approaches in their researches. There seems to be no one universally agreed response in literature in the usage of discourse analysis. For example, Michael Billig, in a chapter in Wetherell et al. (2001), used randomly both linguistic features, identification of "repertoires" (*repertoire* is a coherent way of describing a thing that may be familiar to us but still we fail to notice any difference), and sensitivity to context. Fairclough (1995, 2001), Fairclough and Wodak (1997), and van Dijk (1993) have added to discourse analysis the adjective *critical* to make discourse, "language use in speech and writing," become a form of "social practice." Though Wodak (2001, p. 65) differs in approach, especially with her discourse-historical approach, she sees texts or discourses (historical texts) as having three interrelated perspectives: "discourse immanent critique" (this uncovers the paradoxes and irregularities within the internal structure of the discourse), "socio-diagnostic critique" (this goes to demystify the persuasive or manipulative character of discursive practices), and "prognostic critique" (it sees to the practical application of the findings of the analysis).

CDA Approaches

The approaches of CDA are based on the theoretical levels of sociological and sociopsychological theory. In the tradition of Merton (1967, pp. 39-72), it is summarized as follows (quoted in Meyer and Wodak 2002, pp. 19-20):

a. Epistemology covers theories which provide models of the conditions, contingencies and limits of human perception in general and scientific perception in particular.

b. General social theories, often called "grand theories," try to conceptual-ize relations between social structure and social action and thus link micro- and macro-sociological phenomena . . .

c. Middle-range theories focus either upon specific social phenomena (such as conflict, cognition, social networks), or on specific sub-systems of society (for example, economy, politics, religion).

d. Micro-sociological theories try to explain social interaction, for example the resolution of the double contingency problem (Parsons and Shils 1951, 3-29) or the reconstruction of everyday procedures which members of a society use to create their own social order, which is the objective of ethnomethodology.

e. Socio-psychological theories concentrate upon the social conditions of emotion and cognition and, compared to micro-sociology, prefer causal explanations to hermeneutic understanding of meaning.

f. Discourse theories aim at the conceptualization of discourse as a social phenomenon and try to explain its genesis and its structure.

g. Linguistic theories, for example, theories of argumentation, of grammar, of rhetoric, try to describe and explain the pattern specific to language systems and verbal communication.

Though the seven approaches are interwoven in terms of analyzing discourses, particular attention will be given to "middle-range theories" because Fairclough, whose framework this book is adopting, prefers the middle-range theory position. According to Meyer (2002, p. 22), Fairclough "focuses upon social conflict in the Marxist tradition and tries to detect its linguistic manifestations in discourses, in particular elements of dominance, difference and resistance," and not only that; "he understands CDA as the analysis of the dialectical relationships between semiosis (including language) and other elements of social practices." Van Dijk (2001, p. 352), in his own definition, considers CDA as

> a type of discourse analytical research that primarily studies the way social power abuse, dominance, and inequality are enacted, reproduced, and resisted by text and talk in the social and political context. With such dissident research, critical discourse analysts take explicit position, and thus want to understand, expose, and ultimately resist social inequality.

This poses the question of use of language as an element in social processes. Discourse analysis in itself is a "perspective on social life that contains both methodological and conceptual elements" (Kroger and Wood 2000, p. 3). Thinkers like Althusser (1971, 1995), Bakhtin (2004), Foucault (2003, 2006a), Gramsci (1971), and Habermas (1989) are associated with CDA in one way or another. Hence, CDA is more of an "issue-oriented than theory-oriented" enterprise and its analysis focuses on "better understanding and critique of social inequality, based on gender, ethnicity, class, origin, religion, language, sexual orientation and other criteria that define differences between people" (van Dijk 1997a, pp. 22-23).

This book focuses on conflicts in the conceptions of ideologies that spring from Christian Trinity and Islamic Tawhid as revealed in a common word document. Moreover, it tries to bring out those elements of difference, dichotomy, and power relations that are both covertly and overtly implicated in the constructions of discourses. Some aspects of discourse-historical approach (Wodak 1996) might come into play since its scope also entails examining the truth claims of Tawhid and Trinity respectively. According to Wodak (2002, p. 63), "struggles and contradictions characterize our modern world and . . . nowhere is homogeneity to be found."

Different critical discourse analysts have different traditions. Van Dijk (2002) prefers the sociopsychological side of CDA but relies on sociolinguistic theory which "splints and understands linguistics in a broad 'structural-functional'" sense (Meyer 2002, pp. 2-21). Reisigl and Wodak (2001), with their linguistic-oriented tradition to CDA, understand discourse as "a complex bundle of simultaneous and sequential interrelated linguistic acts" (Meyer 2002, p. 21). But Ron Scollon (2002), who has been a noted micro-sociologist (Meyer 2002) called his approach mediated discourse analysis (MDA), which is associated with CDA. Meyer (2002, p. 23) noted that the overall goal of MDA is, in essence, to link the broad social issues and the everyday talk and writing and to come to a fuller understanding of the history of the practice within the habitus of the participants in a particular social action.

Wodak (2002, p. 65), in trying to make critical discourse analysts free from bias, proposes that they should follow the principle of triangulation. She argues, referring to their works (Wodak et al. 1998, 1999), that "one of the most salient distinguishing features of the discourse-historical approach is its endeavor to work with different approaches, multimethodically and on the basis of a variety of empirical data as well as background information." Discourse as action and interaction as such considers contexts as crucial. For van Dijk (1997b, p. 11), context implies "something we need to know about in order to properly understand the event, action or discourse; something that functions as background, setting, surroundings, conditions or consequences."

Fairclough (1995, p. 2), from another perspective, argues that "the power to control discourse is seen as the power to sustain particular discursive practices with particular ideological investments in dominance over other alternative (including oppositional) practices." Fairclough (1995, pp. 1-2) sets out a framework of reference that is analytical and that studies language in its relation to power and ideology, that views "power as conceptualized both in terms of asymmetries between participants in discourse events, and in terms of unequal capacity to control how texts are reproduced, distributed and consumed (and hence the shapes of texts) in particular sociocultural contexts." In Fairclough's framework, it is argued that the ideologies of the Trinity and Tawhid influence the discourses of both Christians and Muslims and that the forms, contents, and functions of the texts they produce show elements of dichotomy in their relationships as monotheistic religions. Hence, the religious ideals and ideologies they formulate in their different sociocultural contexts are patterned to their discursive practices. Fairclough (2001, p. 235) used the word *genres* as "diverse ways of acting, of producing social life, in the semiotic mode, for example, everyday conversation, meetings in various types of organizations, political and other forms of interview, and book reviews."

Fairclough could be said to have been influenced by Bakhtin (2004), who developed the theory of genre. According to Bakhtin (2004, p. 60),

> language is realized in the form of individual concrete utterances (oral and written) by participants in the various areas of human activity. These utterances reflect the specific conditions and goals of each such area not only through their content (thematic) and linguistic style, that is the selection of the lexical, phraseological, and grammatical resources of the language, but above all through their compositional structure. All three of these aspects— thematic content, style, and compositional structure—are inseparably linked to the whole of the utterance and are equally determined by the specific nature of the particular sphere of communication.

Bakhtin argues that we may call the above *speech genres*. The term *discourses* was used by Fairclough (2001, p. 235) as "diverse representations of social life which are inherently positioned." However, "differently positioned social actors 'see' and represent social life in different ways, as different discourses." Widdowson (1995, 2004) would criticize CDA's use of the term *discourse* as indistinguishable from *text*. He thinks that the term *discourse* in CDA's application is vague even though it is in vogue.

CDA Framework

Using CDA as an analytical framework, this book examines the role of CDA in social transformation and analyzing at the same time the senses of ideologies, hegemonies, differences, similarities, claims to orthodoxy, dichotomies, identity constructions, and misrecognitions as they are used in shaping the religious positions and discourses of Muslims and Christians. It examines the conceptualization of CDA (Fairclough 1992, 1995a, 1995b, 1999, 2000a, 2000b, 2001, 2002, 2004; Fairclough and Wodak 1997; Reisigl and Wodak 2001; van Dijk 1993, 2001; Potter and Wetherell 1987; Wetherell et al. 2001; Taylor 2001a, 2001b; Richardson 2007) and analyzes CDA from the perspective of social transformation (investigating as well Althusser's "ideology as state apparatuses" (1971) and the logic of hegemony [Gramsci 1971, Laclau and Mouffe 1985, Forgacs 1988]).

As religion is incorporated into socio-ethico and legal lives of the Muslim and Christian, the meaning of life and existence are framed from the definitions of their conceptions of God. Therefore, CDA tends to examine how different concepts of the divine, control what Fairclough (2001, p. 235) would call the "order of discourse," which is a "social structuring of semiotic difference—a particular social ordering of relationships amongst different ways of making meaning, i.e., different discourse and genres." Islamic and Christian discourses on God from a semiotic perspective are orders of discourses representing, partly, the socio-ethico and legal lives of both the Muslims and Christians respectively. In such a "structural construction," there exists some marginality and misrecognition or nonrecognition. Here, the word *representation* becomes very important. For "'representation' is a process of social construction of practices, including reflexive self-construction—representations enter and shape social processes and practices" (Fairclough 2001). It helps in the analysis of what happens in texts, their constructions, applications, and implications to authentic communication.

Every individual lives within a "speech community" of a particular humanity, which may be homogeneous or heterogeneous or both. Fairclough (1995a, p. 27) would refer to this kind of "social institution as containing diverse 'ideological-discursive formations'" (IDFs), and thus, he claims that "there is usually one ideological-discursive formation (IDF) which is clearly dominant. For Fairclough (1995a, p. 24) therefore "opposition and struggle are built into the view of the 'order of discourse' of social institutions as 'pluralistic,' each involving a configuration of potentially antagonistic 'ideological-discursive formations' (IDFs), which are ordered in dominance." Each IDF is a sort of "speech community" with its own discursive norms but also, embedded within and symbolized by the latter, its own 'ideological norms.'" Such ideology soon meets some resistance. Fairclough (2001, p. 232) argues that "critical theory and research should seek to address the central problems and issues which face people at a particular point in time." Finding or addressing human problems and issues, he argues, gave vent to the theoretical origins of CDA.

Jurgen Habermas (1989), as argued by Warren (1995), found reason to include everyone in his definitive institution of democracy, which he calls a public sphere. Here, this book attempts to proffer a reason for a common word. Was a common word started for the sake of public sphere between Muslims and Christians? According to Warren (1995, p. 171) "a public sphere is an arena in which individuals participate in discussions about matters of common concern, in an atmosphere free from coercion or dependencies (inequalities) that would incline individuals toward acquiescence or silence."

It is in this guise that this book deciphers the implication of Habermasian "public sphere" on the origination of a common word. Is a common word an arena of decision and organization of action, or is it an arena of decision serving to guide and justify collective actions? (Warren 1995, p. 172). If it is to become an arena of decision serving to guide and justify collective actions, then it is maintaining the same old hegemonic and ideological trend as this book argues below. Examining some methodologies that instantiate language within social relations of hegemony and ideology as tools of oppression, domination, and difference, the Trinitarian and Tawhidic arguments are contextualized. It argues that an analysis of language can lead to a clear understanding of a social life that has been made opaque by hegemony and ideology.

Hegemony

Laclau and Mouffe (1985) considered the transformations of the concept of hegemony as the pivot of their discussion and, at the same time, viewed hegemony as the "discursive surface and fundamental nodal point of Marxist political theorization." In Western Marxism, cultural aspects of social life have been dominated and exploited by particular cultures and ideologies that have been hegemonized. According to Fairclough (2001, p. 232), "the Italian Marxist militant and theorist Antonio Gramsci saw the capitalism of his time (just after the First World War) in terms of a combination of 'political society' and 'civil society'—the former is the domain of coercion, the latter is the domain of what he called 'hegemony.'" It is of this latter domain that this book argues along the line with Laclau and Mouffe (1985) that the "logic of hegemony presented itself from the outset as a *complementary* and *contingent* operation, required for conjectural imbalances within an evolutionary paradigm whose essential or 'morphological' validity was not for a moment placed in question" (quoted in Tallack 1995, p. 341).

Investigating on a type of social action that seeks to transform the social relations that "constructs a subject in a relationship of subordination" (Laclau and Mouffe 1985), there is established synonymity between "subordination," "oppression," and "domination" (quoted in Tallack 1995, p. 343). Laclau and Mouffe argued that by a *relation of subordination*, "an agent is subjected to the decisions of another"; by *relations of oppression*, as a way of contrast to the subordination, "those relations of subordination have transformed themselves into sites of antagonism"; and by *relations of domination* are "the sets of those relations of subordination which are considered as illegitimate from the perspective" (quoted in Tallack] 1995, p. 344). Accordingly, Laclau and Mouffe (1985) argued that "'serf,' 'slave'" do not represent in themselves the antagonistic positions, but these become evident only when "the differential of positivity (the rights inherent to every human being) of these categories can be subverted and the subordination constructed as oppression."

From Laclau and Mouffe (1985) points of view, the Muslims and Christians construe their relations as hegemonic. The Muslim-Christian claims of orthodoxy embedded in relations of insubordination are translated into various forms of antagonism. The eventual effects of insubordination and antagonism following the ideologies of the Tawhid and Trinity are various kinds of specious reasoning. Hegemony emphasizes kinds of power that depend upon consent rather than force (Forgacs 1988, Fairclough 2001). But insubordination, oppression, and domination can be ways of exerting some forces. Hegemony also emphasizes other forms of power that depend upon force rather than consent. For Nietzsche, forces are to generate movements and to create differences. Nietzsche observed two ways of making differences: mastery and slavery. The mastery way of making a difference is affirmative: "I am good, therefore you are evil." While the slavery way is by negation: "You are evil, therefore I am good" (Delueze 1983, pp. 120-121). Hegemonically, this book argues that the Muslim-Christian relation is like a mastery-slavery construct with each trying to outwit the other.

Ideology

Louis Althusser (1971) was very keen in distinguishing the different apparatuses of power. In *Lenin and Philosophy and Other Essays*, Althusser expounded his combination of structuralism and Marxism and presented his criticisms of the humanism of traditional Marxist thought (Sedgwick 2001). His structural Marxism of the State was summarized thus: (1) the state is the repressive state apparatus, (2) state power and state apparatus must be distinguished, (3) the objective of the class struggle concerns state power, and (4) the proletariat must seize state power in order to destroy the existing bourgeois state apparatus (Althusser 1971). Coming from Franco-Marxist philosophy, Althusser viewed ideologies as material social practices in social institutions (churches, parties, trade unions, families, schools, most newspapers) rather than imaginary assemblage (*bricolage*), a pure dream, empty and vain, which is akin to *German Ideology* (quoted in Tallack 1995, pp. 300-305).

Althusser argues that "an ideology always exists in an apparatus, and its practice, or practices," and as such, "Ideological State Apparatuses and their practices become the realization of an ideology (the unity of these different regional ideologies—religious, ethical, legal, political, aesthetic . . . being assured by their subjection to the ruling ideology)" (quoted in Tallack 1995, pp. 307-308). Althusser claims in these theses that (1) there is no practice except by and in an ideology and (2) there is no ideology except by the subject and for subjects (quoted in Tallack 1995, p. 308). Thus, all ideology *interpellates or hails* individuals as subjects.

In the foregoing, it could be said that ideologies of the Tawhid and Trinity are viewed as templates par excellence of the organizational structure of Islam and Christianity. The Tawhidic and Trinitarian ideologies *interpellate or hail* the Muslim and Christian as subjects respectively. For example, in Islam, the testimonies and professions of faith or *Shahadahs* ("There is no god but God, Muhammad is the messenger of God") are the sine qua non of Islam. The professing of these testimonies make one a Muslim, and to deny it makes one a non-Muslim. On the contrary, in Christianity through the sacrament of initiation (baptism), a new member is welcomed into the Christian community. The initiation is ritualized in the name of the Blessed Trinity: God the Father, Son, and Holy Spirit. Through the administration of the sacrament of baptism, someone is made a Christian. Such ideological interpellation of individuals transforms them into subjects. As in the relations between Muslims and Christians, their ideologies have dichotomized the social lives between them.

Pecheux (1982) interpreted Althusser's concept of "discourse" as language from an "ideological perspective, language in the ideological construction of subjects." Besides, Fairclough argues that Bakhtin "proposed the first linguistic theory of ideology," that is, "that linguistic signs (words and longer expressions) are the material of ideology, and that all language use is ideological"; moreover, Bakhtin argues that "any text is explicitly or implicitly in dialogue with other texts (existing or anticipated) which constitutes its 'intertexts'" (Fairclough 2001, p. 233). Michel Foucault, in his books *Madness and Civilization* (2001) and the *Discipline and Punish* (1979), again raised the issue of ideology but from the departure that all knowledge is definable from the perspectives of their relation to power. For him, therefore, "knowledge" and "power" are in interplay ideologically. Foucault maintains that the notion of the subject is basic in every political institution (Foucault 1982, Rabinow 1984, Sedgwick 2001).

Above parlance suggests that the act of defining the individual Muslim or Christian by their respective institutions (Islam or Christianity) makes them subjects under their different religious ideologies. Therefore, discourses could be seen as productive in the sense of having power outcomes. The Christian ideology defines a Christian as someone who is baptized in the name of the Trinity and who follows the teachings of Jesus Christ. Then Islamic ideology defines a Muslim as someone who is either born a Muslim or professes the *Shahadah* in the presence of two or more Muslims.

Criticisms of CDA

CDA is not free from literary critics as being ideological itself. Schegloff criticizes CDA on the grounds that it "has different goals and interests than the local construction of interaction" and that it "should deal seriously with its material: 'If, however, they mean the issues of power, domination and the like to connect up with discursive material, it should be a serious rendering of that material'" (quoted in Meyer 2002, p. 16). Schegloff prefers a CDA that uses conversation analysis as a tool; otherwise, "critical analysis will not 'bind' to the data, and it might end up being ideological." Widdowson (1995) criticized Fairclough's use of CDA as an analytical tool. He argues that the idea of the concept of discourse within CDA is vague, and as such, it does not follow. He further argues that the lack of distinction between text and discourse muddles up the objectivity of CDA and that CDA is a contradiction in terms. However, it is argued that Widdowson has failed to see the reason and effect of the adjective *critical* to discourse analysis. As Scollon (2002) prefers mediated discourse analysis (MDA) and Wodak et al. (1999) and Wodak (2002) would adopt the discourse-historical analysis, so critical discourse analysis is "distinctive in its view of (a) the relationship between language and society, and (b) the relationship between analysis and the practices analyzed" (Fairclough 2004, p. 359).

Adding to his criticisms, Widdowson noted that "CDA is, in a dual sense, a biased interpretation: in the first place it is prejudiced on the basis of some ideological commitment, and then it selects for analysis such texts as will support the preferred interpretation" (quoted in Meyer 2002, p. 17). But it can be said that CDA does not act from bias; rather, it is applied to "discern connections between language and other elements in social life which are often opaque. These include: how language figures within social relations of power and dominion; how language works ideologically" (Fairclough 2001, p. 230). Widdowson might be to a certain extent right with the above criticism of CDA, but CDA is one of the many approaches to data analysis of which its method can be examined in the same context with other linguistic analytic approaches in social relations.

The criticisms leveled against CDA have necessitated some controversies that Meyer (2002, p. 17) termed "'two irreconcilable positions within the methodological debate in social research': Is it possible to perform any research free from *a priori* value judgments and is it possible to gain insight from purely empirical data without using any preframed categories of experience?" This book anticipates the controversies mentioned above, but the Muslim-Christian discourse of a common word is presented as the fundamental object of analysis, but it is not and should not be in itself justifying the different claims.

Data Collection

Fairclough and Wodak (2004)—while giving an example of CDA through an analysis of the extract from a radio interview with Margaret Thatcher, former prime minister of Britain (the interview was conducted by Michael Charlton and was broadcast on BBC Radio 3 on 17 December 1985)—portrayed that there was no set method of data collection. Besides, Fairclough (2001) never gave any methodology of data collection that formed its analysis of the extract of "The Green Paper on Welfare Reform" published by the British (New Labour) Government in March 1998. As observed by Meyer (2002, p. 24),

> whereas Siegfried Jager at least suggests a concentration on texts extracted from television and press reports, no evidence can be found concerning data collection requirements in the contributions of Teun van Dijk and Norman Fairclough. Yet the text examples selected by these authors might indicate that they also prefer mass media coverage.

The idea of van Dijk's and Fairclough's approaches might be summed in the words of Dietmar Janetzko (2008, p. 161) as "*Nonreactive Data Collection*": "hidden, i.e., nonreactive, data collection is of particular interest since it facilitates a non invasive type of research." To unravel the entanglement between religion and society and, of course, to empirically investigate the level of intertwining in the discourses of claims to orthodoxy amongst Muslims and Christians and how they help in constructing both individual and collective identities, this book views the White Paper as "nonreactive" (Janetzko 2008). There are two ways to view the White Paper: its importance and reliability.

It can be said that the Papal Address at the University of Regensburg (September 12, 2006) provoked the interests of Muslim religious leaders/scholars to this landmark *call* to "a common word between us and you." Based on online study of the official website of a common word and through vigorous assessment, there is a collation of different topics from October 13, 2006, when the first *call* to a common word was made to January 1, 2009, after which the website produced its White Paper. In 2009, a whole lot of the collated articles and responses from both Muslims and Christians was in the same website referred to as a White Paper. The method of which the data were collected was based on the online study of the articles, responses, drafts, statements, and conferences and workshops.

Questions about the importance and reliability of the document could be asked. Two criteria make the choice of a common word White Paper a data for analysis. First, it constitutes data for discourse analysis because it belongs to the category of "naturally occurring" texts (Phillips and Hardy 2002), and as such, the collated materials can stand for examples of language in use. The Muslim religious leaders/scholars call for a common word that begins with "An Open Letter and Call from Muslim Religious Leaders to"; of course, Christian religious leaders/scholars responded to the "naturally occurring" texts of the discursive construction of Islamic *valuing, representing,* and *identifying* practices (Fairclough 2001). More so, the Christians' response was not in any way lesser than the Muslims' constructionism. The importance of the "call" for a common word is attached to the necessity for a "public sphere" (Habermas 1989) for both Muslims and Christians. A common word in essence becomes an interfaith initiative that is geared toward bringing together the differences, ideologies, and similarities in Muslim-Christian relations.

The second criterion is reliability. The authenticity of a document is very important in research because it sheds "direct light on important issues concerning the reliability of text as evidence" and emphasis as such has been given to the document's content to the "exclusion of issues of use and function" (Prior 2003, p. 14). Therefore, the reliability of a common word is inundated by its publicity and responses from both Muslim and Christian religious leaders/scholars. They were responses that indicated answers to the "first harmonic" call for togetherness, peace, and sociability. The idea of a common word White Paper is also based on the argument of Blumer (1979, xxiii) that "any research procedure which can tell us something about the subjective orientation of human actors has a claim to scholarly consideration." Documentaries that can tell us something about the human actors include the diaries (Allport 1942, Maas and Kuypers 1974), letters (Thomas and Znaniecki 1958), photographs (Sontag 1978, Curry and Clark 1977, Wagner 1979), films (Calder-Marshall 1963, Rosenthal 1971), and suicide notes (Schwartz and Jacobs 1979). Indeed, a common word White Paper has claim to telling the reader many things about the subjective orientations of human actors involved in it. Furthermore, Prior (2003, p. 2) noted that "the status of things as 'documents' depends precisely on the ways in which such objects are integrated into fields of action, and documents can only be defined in terms of such fields." The fields of action, according to Prior, necessarily involve "creators," "user," and "settings." The White Paper of a common word can be said to be a creation of both Muslims and Christians; it is readily available to anybody who has access to the Internet, and its setting is globally localized.

Fairclough's Analysis Method

Meyer (2002) noted that CDA more or less confines its methodology in hermeneutics than in the analytical-deductive tradition. Hence, different authors have different approaches to data collection as well as data analysis (Fairclough 2002, Jager 2002, Scollon 2002, van Dijk 2002, Wodak 2002). Fairclough (2001) remarked that analytical framework for CDA is modelled upon the critical theorist Roy Bhaskar's concept of "explanatory critique" (Bhaskar 1986, Chouliaraki and Fairclough 2004). Such analytical framework is schematically represented as follows:

Stage 1   Focus upon a social problem that has a semiotic aspect.

Beginning with a social problem rather than the more conventional "research question" accords with the critical intent of this approach—the production of knowledge which can lead to emancipatory change.

Stage 2   Identify obstacles to the social problem being tackled. You can do this through analysis of:

a.) the network of practices it is located within
b.) the relationship of semiosis to other elements within the particular practice(s) concerned
c.) the discourse (the semiosis itself) by means of:
  -   structural analysis: the order of discourse
  -   interactional analysis
  -   interdiscursive analysis
  -   linguistic and semiotic analysis

The objective here is to understand how the problem arises and how it is rooted in the way social life is organized, by focusing on the obstacles to its resolution—on what makes it more or less intractable.

Stage 3   Consider whether the social order (network of practices) "needs" the problem. The point here is to ask whether those who benefit most from the way social life is now organized have an interest in the problem not being resolved.

Stage 4   Identify possible ways past the obstacles. This stage in the framework is a crucial complement to stage 2—it looks for hitherto unrealized possibilities for change in the way social life is currently organized.

Stage 5   Reflect critically on the analysis (Stages 1-4). This is not strictly part of Bhaskar's explanatory critique but it is an important addition, requiring the analyst to reflect on where s/he is coming from, and her/his own social positioning. (Fairclough 2001, p. 236)

As a corollary, Fairclough remarked that the analysis of discourse occurs in "stages 2c and 4," but it is assumed that the analysis of discourse in this book will take place on all the stages. The reason is that in the use of CDA in the investigation of the discourses of both Islamic/Christian religious leaders/scholars, this book examines the texts and reveals how the claims to orthodoxy are produced and reproduced. All the Stages are of paramount importance to this analysis, and that effectively puts emphasis on the realization of authentic communication between Muslims and Christians. It will make use of the five stages in trying to "foreground" the social problems raised in common word White Paper and how they relate to the primary question: How would discourse analysis help in the attempt to authentic communication in Muslim-Christian relations?

CDA methodology was described as analyzing the real and instances of social interaction that takes a linguistic form (Fairclough 2004) though it did not escape the criticisms of Schegloff (1998) and Widdowson (1995, 2004). The CDA methodology was noted as multidimensional since it has no typical data collection procedure (Meyer 2002); this makes a common word document fits in properly to the method of analysis. Using Fairclough's version of CDA (1995, 2001, 2003), the selected texts and associated discursive practices will be examined. Besides, in dealing with Fairclough's analytical framework, the selected texts of a common word are to be examined from the perspectives of lexicon and grammatical markers and modality in the traditions of Carter and McCarthy (2006); Simpson (1993); Carter, Goddard, Reah, Sanger, and Bowring (2005); and Richardson (2007). Again, the selected texts are to be analyzed in the traditions of pictorial art (Yule 1993).

At times, the word of God, for example, in its different scriptures, is made tractable through the texts of the religious leaders/scholars to fit into the ideological norms of religious institutions. When an "ordinary" religious adherent uses or reads the ideologized texts, he or she unintentionally finds himself or herself understanding the text through its ideological meaning. It is argued that readers or religious people should be wary about the functions of "lexemes" (i.e., it "refers to a unit of meaning that may be smaller or larger than the traditional term 'word' implies") (Carter et al. 2005) in discourses. What then constitutes a discourse that could be referred to as interactional? Fairclough (2001, p. 239) refers to interactional analysis as "actual conversations, interviews, written texts, television programs and other forms of semiotic activity." But the difference between "actual conversations" and "written texts" is that in the former, the participants are "co-present in time and space" while in the latter, "there is temporal and spatial distance between them, and the texts acquire a degree of independence both from the writing process and the reading process." Fairclough used the word *text* broadly to include not only written texts but all those forms of discourse mentioned above.

CDA's framework accepts the following representations of interactional analysis as Fairclough argued because it claims that "properties of the text connect with what is going on socially in the interaction," and as such, to make it clear, "what CDA claims is that this connection is interdiscursively mediated: that what is going on socially is, in part, what is going on interdiscursively in the text" (Fairclough 2001, p. 240). Granted that writer/speaker commits himself or herself to discursive practices, he or she unwittingly makes some preponderant texts than what is his or her original intents. But analysis of any texts begins from what the text presents to discourse. Words in texts can take different forms: from being obverse to informing the analyst the implications of connotations and denotations, symmetries and asymmetries, singulars and plurals, words and opposites, present and past, active and passive, diachronic and synchronic. Such a semiotic dualism could be viewed as "simultaneously represent(ing) aspects of the world (the physical world, the social world, the mental world); enact(ing) social relations between participants in social events and the attitudes, desires and values of the participants; and coherently and cohesively connect(ing) parts of texts together" (Fairclough 2003, p. 27).

Texts, in social practices, "are seen as 'work,' as part of productive activity and as part of the process of producing social life." Fairclough (2001, p. 240) insists that they be analyzed both paradigmatically (concerns the range of alternative possibilities available and the choices that are made amongst them in particular texts) and syntagmatically (which concerns the organization or "chaining" of words together in structures [e.g., phrases or sentences]). Thus, texts become "workplace" or the "field" that the dialectic between semiosis and social relations, social identities, and cultural values is played out (Fairclough 2001, p. 241). Textual analysis takes into account the way sentences, phrases, or clauses are structured and the way they are combined especially in the "sequence of sentences" (Fairclough 1995). Fairclough (2001, p. 241) enunciated textual analysis of textual work to include "representing, relating, identifying, valuing." It is argued that the latter are very important for the analysis of the discourses of the Muslim and Christian as they go to examine the differentiating modalities, grammatical markers, and politicized pronouns that are indications of the levels of interactivity going on in Muslim-Christian discourses. Michel Foucault (1990, p. 59), with regard to language in every of its forms, was always suspicious that they do not mean what they say: "The meaning [sens] that one grasps, and that is immediately manifest, is perhaps in reality only a lesser meaning [*moindre sens*] that shields, restrains, and despite everything transmits another meaning, the meaning "underneath it" ["*d'en dessous*"]. This is what the Greeks called *allegoria* and *hyponoia*. Charles Peirce (1931, p. 58) argued that "we think only in signs"; more still, he claims that "nothing is a sign unless it is interpreted as a sign." Again, Foucault (1990, p. 59) anticipates another suspicion in the use of language because, according to him, "there are many other things in the world that speak, and that are not language. After all, it might be that nature, the sea, rustling trees, animals, faces, masks, crossed swords all speak. Perhaps there is some language articulating itself in a way that would not be verbal . . . the semainon of the Greeks." This claim is very crucial especially in trying to distinguish the interdiscursivity of expressions represented in the texts of religious leaders/scholars of both Islam and Christianity.

Linguistic analysis of texts seems to be very similar with the semiotic analysis of texts. A little difference is that "analysis of language is a complex and many-sided process" and "linguistic analysis of texts involves working on the language of a text at various levels" (Fairclough 2001, p. 241). This is so because "discourse as social practice implies a dialectical relationship"; indeed, "a dialectical relationship is a two-way relationship: the discursive event is shaped by situations, institutions and social structures, but it also shapes them" (Fairclough and Wodak 2004, p. 357). In linguistic analysis, Fairclough (2001, pp. 241-242) has an outline of this scheme:

Whole-text language organization—The narrative, argumentative etc. Structure of a text; the way a dialogue is structured.

Clauses combination—The linking of clauses in a complex or compound sentences (i.e., with or without one being subordinated to another); other ways of linking sentences together.

Clauses, i.e., simple sentences—The grammar and semantics of clauses, including categories such as transitivity (transitive or intransitive verbs); verbs relating to action (thought, speech, being, having); voices (active, passive); mood (declarative, interrogative, imperative); modality (degrees of commitment to truth or necessity).

Words—Choice of vocabulary; semantic relations between words (e.g., synonyms, hyponyms); denotative and connotative meaning; collocations (i.e., patterns of co-occurrence); metaphorical uses of words, etc.

In the course of analyzing the data of a common word, it is imperatively assumed that the above analytical framework is methodologically appropriated. CDA can help to locate the route to authentic communication in Muslim-Christian relations. Intertextuality as a concept stipulates that no text is in isolation. Every text is linked up to other texts internally or externally or both. Fairclough very much models his CDA to this type of analysis. Phillips and Jorgensen (2002, p. 70), in their commentary on Fairclough, said that CDA "is based on, and promotes, the principle that texts can never be understood or analysed in isolation—they can only be understood in relation to webs of other texts and in relation to the social context." In applying CDA to the Muslim-Christian discourses, both the internal intertextuality and external intertextuality will be examined. As Richardson (2007, p. 101) noted, internal intertextuality is made up of quotations and reported speeches, and as such, he cited Leitch (1983): "'Prior texts reside in present texts'—indeed all texts consist of, or are composed from, fragments or elements of previous texts." In analyzing the data, it has to be underscored the way quotations and reported speeches cut across religious leaders/scholars' texts and the Qur'anic or biblical texts and how they are chained to the different religious institutions' ideological concepts of God. Externally, Richardson (2007, p. 100) noted that "texts are only fully intelligible . . . when contextualised and 'read' in relation to other texts and other social practices." CDA can be used in the analysis of a common word data from the perspective of what Yule (1993) referred to as the "tradition of pictorial art."

Language as a means of communication has varied traditions of spoken, written, and even pictured discourses. When we look at the cross and the crescent, they are primarily just forms or images that they represent: for the former, two pieces of wood that traversed each other, and the latter, a half-moon. But for centuries, they have come to be likened to the idea of salvation and redemption (for Christianity) and religion. Yule (1993, p. 9) argues that "when some of the 'pictures' came to represent particular images in a consistent way, we can begin to describe the product as a form of picture-writing, or pictograms"; when they take on "more fixed symbolic forms," they are considered as parts of systems "of idea-writing, or ideograms." Religious leaders/scholars could evoke the symbol of the cross or the crescent in the bid to identify the different positions. Yule (1993, p. 9) noted that

> the distinction between pictograms and ideograms is essentially a difference in the relationship between the symbol and the entity it represents. The more "picture-like" forms are pictograms, the more abstract, derived forms are ideograms . . . but they do not represent words or sounds in a particular language.

Thus, he argues that "when symbols come to be used to represent words in a language, they are described as examples of word-writing, or logograms" (1993, p. 10). Therefore, this analytical framework argues that identity could be constructed when pictograms, ideograms, and logograms are used in texts constructions. Here, meaning can become esoteric or ambiguous. The individuals can use pictograms, ideograms, or logograms to create an identity that dichotomizes in an unintentional or intentional way.

Through modality, the meanings of texts can be examined or analyzed. For Simpson (1993, p. 47), "modality refers broadly to a speaker's attitude towards, or opinion about, the truth of a proposition expressed by a sentence. It also extends to their attitude towards the situation or event described by a sentence." The modality of the texts together with the disposition or orientation of the speaker/writer, all contribute to the formation of the discourse of the texts. For Richardson (2007, p. 59), "modality provides a further step in our analysis, showing that there are not only links between *form* and *content*, but also between *content* and *function*." Modality refers further to statements that make categorical assertions, and it shows that the knowledge between the writer and reader are clear-cut (Fairclough 2001); therefore, the knower tells the uninformed about the known. Richardson (2007) noted that modality, which is indicated through the modal verbs, could have some negations. Assessing the usage of modal verbs in the construction of identity in terms of Muslim-Christian relations goes a long way to open up the kind of relationship that is going on or that is expected to go on between the individual Muslim and Christian. The utterances of religious leaders/scholars can create ideological loophole. Fairclough (2003) argues that modality, in view of "what authors commit themselves to," and evaluation, "what is desirable or undesirable," are pertinent indications of how identifications are produced. He further argued elsewhere that

> whereas analysis of orders of discourse tries to specify the semiotic resources available to people (the social structuring of semiotic diversity), interactional analysis is concerned with how those resources interact, that is, the active semiotic work that people are doing on specific occasions using those resources. (2001, p. 240)

The modal verbs as indicated below help in the analysis of the "content" and "function" of texts. Carter et al. (2005, p. 143) argued that "whenever instructions are given, a modality enters the relationship between the writer and reader of a text." Modal verbs can take any form within a particular text. It could take the form of *mode of reassurance/possibility* (e.g., *may* cause an interruption, every effort *will* be made) or *mode of control* (e.g., *must* be boiled before drinking, *can* continue to be used) (2005, p. 145). They can even take the form of *mode of predictions/intentions* (Carter and McCarthy 2006). Examples of this mode can be located in these: "Say: O People of the Scripture! Come to a common word between us and you: that we *shall* worship none but God" (Al-'Imran 3:64). Another is "Hear, O Israel, the Lord our God, the Lord is One! And you *shall* love the Lord your God with all your heart" (Deuteronomy 6:4).

Because of the "content" and "function" of modality, it is further expressed in two principal forms, namely, truth modality and obligation (or duty) modality.

> Truth modality varies along a scale of options from the absolutely categorical . . . through to varying degrees of hedging . . . and reduced certainty . . . . Obligation modality refers to future events and, specifically, the degree to which the speaker/writer believes that a certain course of action or certain decisions *ought* or *should* be taken. (Richardson 2007, p. 60)

Modality could be assessed from other verbs that give similar meanings to full modal verbs. For Carter and McCarthy (2006), *is to, are to,* and *ought to* are referred to as semimodal verbs. For example, the semimodal verb *ought to* gives the same *mode of obligation* as *should*. Modality could also be indicated through adverbs like *certainly, truly, frankly, honestly* (Richardson 2007). Modal adverbials are in patterns. They can be used in linking, circumstantial, or by way of stance (Biber et al. 2002). Adverbials help in deciphering the speaker/ writer's point of departure, general emotional or intellectual disposition, or the spatio-temporal conditionality that influences the texts.

When somebody is referred to by his or her title, it creates some awareness between the reader and writer/speaker. In discourse, *title* and *titling* could be observed from the point of view of the speaker/writer, from the spatio-temporal conditionality of the event, and the context of the texts. *Title* is to be distinguished from *titling*. The former is the noun form of the name appellation that goes with an individual's full name. The latter is derivative from the verb form. It is an act of giving the individual or calling the individual by that *title*. The former is *inert*, while the latter evokes some awareness of *agency*; it puts some *consciousness* on the titleholder. Thus, when the title *His Holiness* or *Imam* is used in a text, Richardson (2007) argues that they are range of identities that signify roles and characteristics that could be used to describe the people with the above appellations accurately, but in the text, they could have different meanings. "The manner in which social actors are named identifies not only the group(s) that they are associated with (or at least the groups that the speaker/ writer *wants* them to be associated with) it can also signal the relationship between the namer and the named" (2007, p. 49). In analyzing how the texts relate to the ideologies of the Tawhid and Trinity, *title* and *titling* are considered especially when *title* is construed as *inertia*, that is, the "disinclination to act," and *titling* is the act of evoking the agency of consciousness. Besides, *title* and *titling* in the context of the Muslim leaders' open letter and call to Christian religious leaders could be interpreted as a category of a group of individuals that take others for Lords beside God (Yusuf'Ali 2008, p. 144). *Titling* could also designate functions and acknowledgment of nobility. Richardson (2007, p. 49), citing Blommaert (2005, p. 11), remarked that

> apart from referential meaning, acts of communication produce *indexical* meaning: social meaning, interpretative leads between

what is said and the social occasion in which it is being produced. Thus the word "sir" not only refers to a male individual, but it *indexes* a particular social status and the role relationships of deference and politeness entailed by this status.

Again the pronouns (such as *I, he, she, it, we, they, you*) "are the main means of identifying speakers, addressees and others" (Carter et al. 2005, p. 134). Inasmuch as they play the role of "identifying speakers, addressees and others," they also limit the level of monotony in constant repetitions of names. At other times, they can be politically used to manipulate discourses. Carter et al. (2005, p. 194) used the phrase *the politics of pronouns* to assert that

> it's important to realise that grammatical structures are not simply neutral—they are intimately related to power: for example, pronoun reference in a text is all about who is in the picture and how they're being seen, as well as about helping to construct a particular kind of relationship between writer and reader. These are issues of power, because written texts are a powerful source of information for us about the nature of our world—not just the physical world, but our social, political and emotional "realities" too.

The White Paper that forms the analysis of this study foregrounds pronouns, especially in the phrase *a common word between us and you*. It is argued that the phrase is raveled in mystery. Through CDA, the wide gap between *us Muslims* and *you Christians* will be noted, and at the same time, it will unravel the connectivity between the truth claims of both Muslims and Christians. Carter et al. (2005, pp. 194-195), emphasizing on the politics of pronouns, noted that the pronoun *one* has been used as a "neutral way to refer simply to a 'person' without specifying a sex for them"; but it "can carry suggestions of pretension," and *they* has equally been used generically when people are referred to generally or "a person of unspecified sex." *They* has also been used to refer to "a person of either sex." The pronoun *you*, Carter et al. (2005, p. 195) claimed, has had a "directly political history." They noted that "originally, English had two forms of 'you': 'thou'/'thee' was used to one person, and 'ye'/'you' for group address. 'Thou' (*singular*) was used when the person was the subject of the sentence, and 'thee' (*singular*) for the object; similarly, 'ye' (*plural*) was used for the subject, 'you' (*plural*) for the object" (*italics* mine). Besides, the *you* not only represent the singular or plural address; Carter et al. (2005, p. 196) argued that it "came to mark the relationship between people." The diagram below represents the relationships.

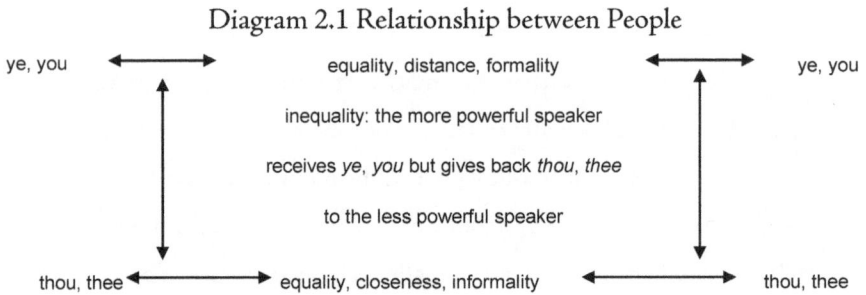

Diagram 2.1 Relationship between People

| ye, you | ⟷ | equality, distance, formality | ⟷ | ye, you |

inequality: the more powerful speaker

receives *ye, you* but gives back *thou, thee*

to the less powerful speaker

| thou, thee | ⟷ | equality, closeness, informality | ⟷ | thou, thee |

(Source: Adapted from Carter et al. 2005)

The diagram 2.1 above portrays the kind of communication that goes on through the pronouns *ye, you, thou, thee*, which enforces some power relations of equality, intimacy, proximity, and distance. Carter et al. (2005, p. 196) argued that

> if people who were social equals were addressing each other, the plural forms could be used between the individuals (i.e., as singular forms) to signal distance and formality, while the singular forms could signal closeness and intimacy when used reciprocally; if the people were not equals, however, the plural forms could be used in addressing the more powerful person, as a mark of respect and

authority, while the singular forms could be used in addressing the less powerful person to mark low status.

Therefore, in analyzing the discourse of both Islamic and Christian religious leaders/scholars, the politics of pronouns will be examined carefully so that in their usage, the implications of what van Dijk referred to as "ideological squares" and how the pronouns can be used discriminatorily in the discourse of Muslim-Christian relations will be brought to the fore.

Moreover, Carter et al. (2005, p. 78), as noted above, introduced the term *lexeme* to show a distinction between a *lexeme* and the traditional term *word*. They argued that

> meaning . . . exists in units of language smaller than the word, in morphemes. Users of English frequently use the term "word" when, strictly speaking, they are referring to morphemes. If someone looks a word up in the dictionary, for example "dogs," they don't look up the plural form, they look up the base morpheme "dog."

Thus, morpheme adds new meaning to a particular "word." Below, the examination of the kinds of morpheme will give further understanding in the discourses of Muslims and Christians as constituting series of actions that structure identity or forms that maintain the status quo.

Morphemes are apparently identifiable in any propositions. They are established in units smaller than words. For example, the term *pater* has one morpheme, but the term *paternal* (pater-nal) has two morphemes while the term *paternity* (pater-ni-ty) has three morphemes. They are all terms from one root but have different meanings. Carter et al. argued that morphemes can be differentiated in two ways: Free morphemes can "constitute words by themselves: pig, bark, like." Bound morphemes are "only used as parts of words: s, ed, un, ship." Also, the bound morphemes have two functions:

The inflectional morphemes "act as grammatical marker, giving information about number, verb tense, aspect and other grammatical functions." Examples of these include "-s, -ed, -er (comparative), -es." Then the derivational morphemes help to "form new words." Examples include "un-, -li, -hood, -y, dis-, -ship, -er (to create a noun of agency)" (see Carter et al. 2005, pp. 77-78). If CDA uses morphemes as conceptual tool in analyzing the terms like *Muslim-Christian relation(s)* and *Muslim-Christian relationship(s)*, it asks the question, Is it a "relation(s)" and/or "relationship(s)" that constitute a series of actions that preempt identity or a structure or form that seeks to maintain the status quo?

Figurative expressions often draw the attention of the reader to the purpose of any text. Different language and text organization can be used to get the message across to the reader. This is what figures of speech do. Figures of speech like metaphor, metonym, hyperbole, simile in a text portray that text as rich in imagery because they tend to represent objects, subjects, actions, or ideas. This analytical framework appropriates this conceptual tool as well because it is assumed that the discourses of Muslims and Christians adopt some of these linguistic features in order to maintain sustained argumentations of the different monotheistic ideologies. Richardson (2007, p. 67) examines some of these figures of speech as well as citing Reisigl and Wodak (2001) and Fairclough (2000). Below they are summarized as:

Metaphor: this is "perceiving one thing in terms of another," for example, "*Word* of God."

Hyperbole: this is an "example of excessive exaggeration made for rhetorical effect."

Metonym: "a metonym is a trope in which one word, phrase or object is substituted for another from a semantically related field of reference."

Briefly, Richardson (2007, p. 68), citing Reisigl and Wodak (2001, pp. 56-58), gave a way of how metonyms can act as substitutes that act as the anchor of analyzing a common word. For instance, when

-the cause or creator is replaced by the product: e.g., "the Anti-terrorism, Crime and Security Act 2001 criminalises Muslims";

-the user of an object replaced by the object: e.g., "Rachel Corrie was killed by an Israeli bulldozer";

-people replaced by a place in which these people work/are staying: e.g., "The White House declared...";"the detention centre erupted into violence";

-events replaced by the date on which these events occurred: e.g., "September 11th must never be allowed to occur again";

-a country, or state replaced by (certain) people living in this country: e.g., "We cannot let evil of ethnic cleansing stand. We must not rest until it is reversed" ([Tony Blair 22 April 1999] quoted in Fairclough 2000, p. 148).

Chapter Three

Analysis of A Common Word

In this chapter, the analysis of a common word is made. It does that via "Stage 1: Locating the Social Problems in the Research Question," that is, the primary question of the relationship that make authentic communication between Muslims and Christians very difficult, and "Stage 2: Identifying the Problems to Be Tackled." Besides, it makes an interactional analysis of the White Paper.

Stage 1: Locating the Social Problems in the Research Question

The way both the Muslim and Christian experience each other in terms of behavior and interaction has been one full of suspicions and even utter condemnation of each other's religious beliefs. A critical look at *surah Al-Ikhlas* 112 will give some clues to the kind of problems that make it very difficult to form Muslim-Christian relationships based on the ideologies of the Tawhid and Trinity. Analyzing *surah Al-Ikhlas* 112 from the perspectives of Rodwell's translation (1994) and Al-Hilali and Khan's translations (1996), a clear line is drawn between them. For Rodwell, who has European influence, the *surah* reads, "SAY: He is God alone: God the eternal! He begetteth not, and He is not begotten; And there is none like unto Him." Rodwell's translation has no footnotes or any commentaries to this *surah* (112). However, the Saudi-sponsored English translation—*The summarized in one volume of the Qur'an' (Interpretation of the Meanings of the Noble Qur'an in the English Language)*—of Al-Hilali and Khan rendition has some footnotes and commentaries from *Hadith* and *tafsir* embellishing *surah Al-Ikhlas* 112: "Say (O Muhammad . . .): He is Allah, (the) One."

Here, the Al-Hilali and Khan translation have a very long footnote expounding the concept of *Tawhid* (monotheism) that was linked to the glossary. Then verse two of the same *surah* (*Al-Ikhlas* 112) continues, "Allah-us-Samad . . . [Allah the Self-Sufficient Master Whom all creatures need (He neither eats nor drinks)]. He begets not, nor was He begotten." *Hadith* number 470 was quoted to substantiate this verse.

> Narrated Mu'adh bin Jabal . . . : The Prophet . . . said, "O Mu'adh! Do you know what Allah's Right upon slaves is? I said, "Allah and His Messenger know better." The Prophet . . . said, "To worship Him (Allah) Alone and to join none in worship with Him (Allah). Do you know what their right upon Him is? I replied, "Allah and His Messenger know better." The Prophet . . . said, "Not to punish them (if they did so)." (Sahih Al-Bukhari, vol. 9, *Hadith* no. 470)

Hadith numbers 471, as noted by Sahih Al-Bukhari (vol. 9) narrated by Abu Sa'id Al-Khudri, and 472, narrated by 'Aisha, are all in consonance with *Hadith* number 470. The last verse of *surah Al-Ikhlas* 112 says, "And there is none co-equal or comparable unto Him."

It could be argued that the Saudi-sponsored English translation of the Qur'an was ideologically framed with emphasis on points of conflicts between Islam and Christianity. If the above is taken wholesale by Muslims, then authentic communication between the two religious communities will be very difficult.

Consequently, the Christians (Trinitarian Christianity) would reply to the Qur'anic denunciation ("He begets not, nor was He begotten. And there is none co-equal or comparable unto Him") of Jesus Christ by polemically referring to Islam as a heresy and Muhammad and Muslims as heretics. John Damascene (675-753), for example, critically denounced Islam in his *The Heresy of the Ishmaelites* and *A Dialogue between a Christian and a Saracen.* Chapman noted that (1998, p. 87):

> John treated Islam as a Christian heresy, rather than as a religion in
> its own right. This was understandable, since he probably thought
> Islam was a passing heresy that would not survive for very long.
> It meant, however, that he was constantly comparing Islam with
> Christianity, and therefore hardly able to think himself into the
> minds of Muslims.

Again, Peter Venerable (1094-1156) was famous for his treatises *Summa totius haersis Saracenorum* (Summary of all the heresies of the Saracens) and *Liber Contra sectam sive haeresim Saracenorum* (A book against the heresy of the Saracens). In these treatises, Peter construed Islam as a totality of Christian heresies. He saw Muhammad to have been schooled by a Christian, a Nestorian Monk—Bahira. This same monk later converted him and made him a Nestorian Christian. He considered Muhammad's teachings as combinations of Judaism, Manicheanism and Nestorianism. Since Muslims do not regard the sacraments, though they regard the prophets and Jesus, Peter viewed them as arch heretics (Kritzeck 1964, pp. 129-144). Though it is not the scope of this book to discuss the Christian Crusades and Islamic Crescentades, the several Christian attacks and counterattacks by Muslims in the Middle Ages and the consequent imbroglios over the Holy Land (Jerusalem) also added to the social problems that deteriorate relationship between Muslims and Christians.

In recent times, the so-called war on terror has been construed as a Western machination to control the Muslim population. West (Rienstra and Tranchet 2008) here supposedly refers to Christianity because of its root in Christian values. It is fallacious to refer to Christianity as a religion when Western nations are pursuing politically things that matter to their national interests. Christianity is beyond the territories of the regional Western Hemisphere. As Islam is not restricted only to Middle East, Christianity is not restricted to the West only. The crux of this analysis is the problem of different religious claims to orthodoxy that follows from their different definitions of *monotheism*—Tawhid and Trinity. Therefore, in analyzing the White Paper, this book contextualizes the problems of difference between the ideologies of the Tawhid and Trinity and views them as influencing the later social actions and interactions between Muslims and Christians. Stage 2 emphasizes the need to identify the problems to be tackled and the CDA approaches to the texts.

Stage 2: Identifying the Problems to Be Tackled

The entire White Paper will be articulated through a bird's-eye view at this stage. Besides, in this same stage, the discursive practices of the White Paper will be analyzed by means of structural analysis (the order of discourse), interactional analysis, interdiscursive analysis, and linguistic and semiotic analysis in order to bring the problems of ideologies, dichotomies, claims to orthodoxy, and differences that are encrypted into the different texts. Under linguistic and semiotic analysis, it will not only use Fairclough's schemes (2001) in terms of whole-text language organization, clauses combination, clauses, and words, analytical method. From the perspectives of lexicon and grammatical markers in the traditions of Carter and McCarthy (2006); Simpson (1993); Carter, Goddard, Reah, Sanger, and Bowring (2005), and Richardson (2007), these extracts are analyzed as well. Again, the selected texts are to be analyzed in the traditions of pictorial art (Yule 1993).

In dealing with the extracts from the White Paper, this book is particularly interested in how the different discourses are channeled to foreground the definitions of the orthodoxy claims of Tawhid and Trinity. Importance is given to the way the different texts are structured—whether the texts are dialogical, reactionary, or responsive. It will observe at the same time the use of pronouns in terms of Muslim-Christian relations. It will look at the clause combination—whether they are paratactic (the placing of clauses side by side in a sentence without the use of conjunctions) or hypotactic (the subjunction of one clause to the other by the use of conjunctions) and to examine the clauses used (the perspectives of verbs, adjectives, nouns, mood and modality of the sentences.) Moreover, this book will, at the same time, examine the choice of words used in the discourses: the synonyms, polysemys, antonyms; the denotative and connotative meanings; collocations and metaphorical and metonymical uses of words (Fairclough 2001, Reisigl and Wodak 2001, Richardson 2007).

Interactional Analysis of the White Paper

Based on an online study (October 10, 2006-January 6, 2009) of *The Official Website of A Common Word* (see OWACW 2007), the White Paper is made up of collated articles, responses from both Islamic and Christian religious leaders, scholars, intellectuals, and professionals. It is also comprised of addresses, communiqués, final statements, press releases, and speeches. The whole lot gathered together makes it a solemn tome of 294 pages.

Initially, "a common word between us and you" was designed as an "open letter" and "call" from Muslim religious leaders to Christian religious leaders in October 13, 2007. The phrase *open letter* does not sound like a term suggesting interfaith dialogue. It is more of a letter of protest addressed to Christian religious leaders that was made public. It was a letter that attracted or was designed to attract media attention and the world public opinion. The word *call* in its ambiguous usage can suggest a kind of summon to some particular offices or professions. Thus, the social structuring of semiotic differences (genres and discourses) constitute the order of discourse of the White Paper (Fairclough 2001).

The introduction pages of the White Paper claim some accomplishments made by a common word between 2007 and 2008. It claims among other things in the "Frequently Asked Questions" (FAQ) that it has become the world's leading interfaith dialogue initiative between Muslims and Christians specifically, and also it has become an interfaith theological document based on two Qur'anic and biblical commandments: love of God and love of neighbor. There is a gap between "dialogue" and an "open letter" or a "call." An "open letter" sounds more like a letter of protest. It is not clear whether a protest was being promoted, but the sandwich of the idea of world peace hanging on the balance should Muslims and Christians continue to live at daggers' drawn is very imperative. Moreover, other prospective audiences of the White Paper are Muslims and Christians globally.

Table 3.1 shows the various dates of the different genres, the topics, and summaries. The reason for the schematic illustration is to give a heuristic guide to when each of the genres was developed and to indicate how the primary question, *How would discourse analysis help in the attempt to authentic communication in Christian-Muslim relations?* is applied in deconstructing the social problems serialized in the discourses of the White Paper.

Table 3.1 Heuristic Guide to *A Common Word* 'White Paper' Booklet 2008

No.	Date	Genre	Discourse
1	13/10/06	An Open Letter to the Pope "A Common Word Between Us and You"	This was an open letter of invitation from initially 38 Muslim scholars to the Christian representatives for an understanding that is based on love of God and love of neighbor, which is derived from the unicity of God.
2	2007-2008	A Common Word Accomplishments	Signatories of both Christians and Muslims to the response of the call; claims of achievements in terms over 600 articles written in English on A Common Word, subject of MA and MPhil dissertations in Harvard University, University of Tubingen, and the Centre for Studies of Islam, UK. Subject of International conferences in USA and UK.
3	13/10/07	Expansion on Their Message to the Pope et al., "A Common Word Between Us and You"	Expansion on their message with added Muslim scholars and leaders' signatories in support of "A Common Between Us and You" with serious emphasis on the testimonies of faith.
4	13/10/07	Response by Professor David Ford, Director of Cambridge Interfaith Programme	Listed three reasons why the call is important: (i) it influences in bringing together different Islamic religious authorities and scholars together and uniting them in a positive, substantial way; (ii) it addresses Christianity in a friendly word and seeks to engage with the Christian Scriptures respectfully and carefully; (iii) it opens a way forward that is more practicable and provides a kind of public sphere.
5	13/10/07	Response by former British Prime Minister Right Hon. Tony Blair	Acknowledges that *A Common Word* proposition is the only way in the modern times of making sense of different history and culture. He prefers both Christians and Muslims identifying themselves by reference to a shared future to differences.

6	13/10/07	Response of over 300 leading Christian scholars to "A common Word Between Us and You"	Christian leaders and scholars reply to "A Common Word Between Us and You" based also on "loving God and neighbor together."
7	15/10/07	Response by the World Alliance of Reformed Churches	In acknowledging the need for the common word, they remarked that several efforts have been made in planning interfaith meetings especially around the conflicts in parts of Indonesia.
8	05/11/07	Response of the Mennonite Church	They welcome the suggestion that emphasizes that Christians and Muslims agree to some important theological and ethical foundations in common and respect as well; they call for a genuine Christian-Muslim dialogue.
9	18/03/08	Response by Rev. Dr. Samuel Kobia	In his message, he noted that World Council of Churches agreed that the complex history of Christian-Muslim relations has been dotted with much rivalry and war; there were still rich and fertile encounters at the level of life and ideas alike.
10	02/04/08	Response from Archbishop Yeznik Petrosyan—Press Release of the Mother See of Holy Etchmiadzin	Welcomes the expression of goodwill from Islamic religious leaders/scholars who argues for peace and fraternal love promotion among the leaders and faithful of the monotheistic religions of the world.
11	14/04/08	Response by His Holiness Patriarch Alexy II of Moscow and all Russia	He claims that Christians and Muslims have similar aims, but in achieving them, there is a need for them to clarify their understanding of each other's religious values.
12	14/07/08	Archbishop of Canterbury, detailed response to "A Common Word"	Archbishop argues that "A Common Word" should translate into common good.

13	24/07/08-31/07/08	Loving God and Neighbor in Word and Deed: Implications for Christians and Muslims—Workshop and Conference, Yale University, USA	The workshop and conference rose with a four-count final statement: (i) affirming the unity and absoluteness of God; (ii) recognizing that all human beings have rights to the preservation of life, religion, property, intellect and dignity; (iii) a commitment to furthering the basic principles of love through steady dialogue; (iv) denouncing the threats made against those who engage in interfaith dialogue.
14	12/10/08-15/10/08	A Common Word and Future Muslim-Christian Engagement, Conference, University of Cambridge and Lambeth Palace, UK	The conference as well rose with a four-count final communiqué: (i) to identify and promote the use of educational materials for all peoples as ways of providing fair reflection of their faiths; (ii) to build a network of academic institutions that will link scholars, students, and academic resources; (iii) to identify funds to facilitate exchanges between trainees for role leadership in Christianity and Islam; (iv) to translate pertinent texts of both Christian and Islamic traditions for the use of the other.
15	04/11/08-06/11/08	Love of God, Love of Neighbor: First Seminar of the Catholic-Muslim Forum, Conference, Rome, Italy	The conference rose with a fifteen-count final declaration that was a summary of the themes of love of God and neighbor.
16	04/11/08	Speech by His Eminence, The Grand Mufti of Bosnia, Sheikh Mustafa Ceric, Catholic-Muslim Forum, Rome	His emphasis was on the shared values between Christianity and Islam: share life together; share the clay from which mankind was formed; share belief in one God; share the same father, Adam, and the same mother, Eve; share air; share Abrahamic faith; share love and respect for the Blessed Virgin Mary (Maryam) and Jesus (Isa) her son.

17	06/11/08	Response by His Holiness Pope Benedict XVI—Address to Participants in the First Catholic-Muslim Forum, Rome	He emphasized on the theme of love of God and neighbor. He claims that love is the reason God created the universe, and through his love, he becomes present in human history (definitely in Jesus Christ). He remarked that God came down to meet man and, while remaining God, took on human nature. Though the Christian-Islamic anthropological and theological visions separate them, both should work together in promoting genuine respect for the dignity of the human person and rights.
18	06/11/08	"We and You—Let Us Meet in God's Love," Address by Professor Seyyed Hossein Nasr, Catholic-Muslim Forum, Rome	This address is redolent of pronoun phrases notably in politics of pronoun: "we and you," "we both," "both us and you," "we Muslims," "you and us," "both our."
19	10/11/08	Response by His Beatitude Chrisostomos, Archbishop of Cyprus	Agrees that monotheism and love of the other are the common fundamental values of Christianity and Islam, which compel both to root out the causes of violence, war, destruction of the environment, starvation, the violation of human rights. He also observes the religious and theological differences of both Christianity and Islam.
20	22/11/08	"A Common Word" wins Germanys Eugen Biser Foundation—Speech by Prince Ghazi	An articulation of the reasons for A common word.

21	23/12/08	Response by the Baptist World Alliance	Embraces the convictions of Muslim religious leaders/scholars that love of God and neighbor will help in resolving the huge needs for peace, justice, and love in the world today. He refers to Trinity and unity of God as diverging points between Christianity and Islam and seeks to explore the way in which both occupy the common ground from their different orientations.
22	05/01/09	United Methodist Council of Bishops' Response to "A Common Word Between Us and You"	They believe that God created all people in his own image. They affirm what they have in common with people of all faiths, though different in many ways. Ever ready to identify the shared theological concepts, moral teachings, and spiritual disciplines.
23	06/01/09	Response by Rev. Dr. Mark S. Hanson, Presiding Bishop of the Evangelical Lutheran Church in America and President of the Lutheran World Federation	Encourages through prayer and supports the planning for communities of justice, peace, and security as wellspring of recourse for the monotheistic religions.
24	-	Frequently Asked Questions (FAQ)	Here, the origin, reason, authorship, aims, and objectives of *A Common Word* was established.

The compilation of the different genres that form a common word White Paper gives it the credential as data for social research. This book selects particular texts from the document for analysis. It goes to the point where it all began. Thus, the initial "*An Open Letter and Call from Muslim Religious Leaders to*" is the first extract to be analyzed. The reason for using it at the beginning of this analysis is that it introduced particularly the arguments that overwhelmed the ideological stances of Tawhidic claims. These—the official call in terms of an open letter from Muslim religious leaders, the Christian response, and the fifteen-point declaration of the Catholic-Muslim Forum—are in the appendices.

Chapter Four

An Open Letter and Call

An open letter and call from the Muslim religious leaders to their Christian counterparts is called extract 1. Based on Fairclough's analytical framework, it makes a summary of extract 1 in the form of interactional analysis; it continues with the interdiscursive analysis, linguistic analysis (examining the whole-text organization), clause combination, clauses, and words. The White Paper, a common word between *us* and *you*, raises the issue of difference; the difference is very apparent in the pronouns used—*us* and *you*. It proposes that love of God and love of neighbor are the "basis for peace and understanding" between Muslims and Christians. On the issue of difference, the White Paper further raises the issue of representation, the representation of a particular concept of monotheism—*Tawhid*.

According to the analytical framework, there is a need to establish whether the social order needs the problem of representation (Fairclough 2001). Inasmuch as the White Paper is ensuing for peace and interfaith dialogue, it also strategizes a Tawhidic preference. Hence, extract 1 begins with the words "*An Open Letter and Call from Muslim Religious Leaders to*"[4] (see appendix A). Arguably, it may be said that the text was seeking space for dialogue between Islam and Christianity, but its denouement in the phrase *open Letter* and the word *call* suggests a letter made public and also a letter meant to be a protest.

There are some ambiguities surrounding the language use of the phrase *open letter*. Was the open letter (protest) against the Papal Address at the University of Regensburg? Was it against the Christian understanding of monotheism? Here, it considers the "open letter" text as a "protest" both to the Papal Address and to Christian concept of monotheism. Perusing through extract 1, there is so much emphasis on the Qur'anic argument against "associating partners to God," which often is directly an attack on Christianity (see appendix A). For example, paragraph 10 of extract 1 says,

> Say: O People of the Scripture! Come to a common word between us and you: that we shall worship none but God, and that we shall ascribe no partner unto Him, and that none of us shall take others for lords beside God. (*Al-'Imran* 3:64)

It could be said that the document was aimed at the public domain, both Muslims and Christians in particular, but to the larger society as well. The phrase *open letter* is a way of *identifying* the document. There are two senses to it. First, the intended audience of extract 1 was not limited to the Christian Church leaders; hence, the letter was published late 2007 in *The New York Times* and in *The Official Website of A Common Word* (see OWACW 2007). Second, it could be argued further that the letter was intended as an official interpretation of Islamic belief that cedes no compromise. As question number 25 of the FAQ asked,

Is this document just another form of propaganda? If you mean by
that witnessing and proclaiming one's faith with compassion and
gentleness, then yes. If you mean forcing one's views on others, then
no. (see ACWWP 2008)

Indeed, a common word document as portrayed in the FAQ can be used
to propagandize one's faith. If by propaganda it is understood as an organized
way to spread the message of one's faith, which may destroy the cause of the
avowed objective of a common word, then it is a form of mission, or *da'wa*,
to attract the attention of the global Muslim audience. Below is the summary
of the analysis of extract 1.

Summary of Extract 1: Interactional Analysis

Extract 1 comprises of 56 paragraphs (see appendix A) identified by
this book for quick reference. Here, they are arranged into paragraphs in this
systematic way. Paragraph 1 begins with flushed left and a tab indentation.
Then paragraphs 2-7 are flushed left with no indentation. Paragraphs 8-56
are justified, and each paragraph begins with a tab indentation.

Paragraph 1 introduces with the festival of *Eid al-fitr al-Mubarak* 1428
AH/October 13, 2007 CE.

Paragraphs 2-7 contains the titles and names of some Christian hierarchies
who were sent the "open letter" and "call."

Paragraph 8 sees the construction of world peace as conditionally based
on sustenance of peace and justice between Muslims and Christians.

Paragraph 9 gives the fundamental principles of both faiths: love of God
and love of neighbor.

Paragraph 10 is the Qur'anic citation of the call to "a common word
between us and you" (*Al-'Imran* 3:64).

Paragraphs 11-12 give a brief explanation of the call to "a common word."

Paragraphs 13-14 cite a call unto the way of the Lord and the injunction to vie with them in the fairest of way.

Paragraph 15 begins the first part of "a common word between us and you." Here, love of God in Islam is emphasized.

Paragraphs 16-27 are the expositions of the love of God, and they maintain the unity of God (a common word document shifts from being a project offering ideas to new relations between Muslims and Christian. It becomes evaluative, sustaining the argumentation of the ideology of Tawhid).

Paragraphs 28-30 expound further on the unity of God and claim that the profession of faith in these words: "There is no god but God," a "blessed formula and nothing can be better than that."

Paragraphs 31-39 present love of God referenced to the Bible as the first and greatest of commandments. There is a wide gap of difference in the expressions love of God in "Islam" and Love of God in the "Bible." If love of God can be found in Islam, can it not be found in Christianity? Why not love of God in Christianity? Why the Bible?

Paragraphs 40-42 are the second part of the open letter: love of the neighbor in Islam.

Paragraphs 43-45 present love of the neighbor in the Bible. The problem noted in paragraphs 31-39 is equally spotted in paragraphs 43-45.

Paragraphs 46-47 are the part 3: Come to a Common Word Between Us and You. These paragraphs emphasized on the unity of God.

Paragraphs 48-53 are very imperative to the basis of "a common word." Refers back to *Al-'Imran* 3:64, citing the Qur'an, Tafsir, the Bible, Christians, and exegetes.

Paragraphs 54-56, Between Us and You, draw some conclusions that reemphasized the need for peace and the impending cataclysmic outcome if neglected.

What each of the paragraphs keep informing the reader is the problem of difference between *us* and *you* and the "foregrounding" of the concept of

Tawhid. The FAQ claims that a common word document has become "the world's leading interfaith dialogue initiative between Christians and Muslims specifically, and also it has become an interfaith theological document" (see ACWWP 2008). Therefore, interfaith dialogue has also been "foregrounded." In analyzing extract 1, emphasis shall be on textual "work" of Fairclough's framework of "relating, representing, identifying and valuing" (2001). Emphasis again will be on the discourses as presented and at the same time representing different positions between *us* and *you*. This will bring into focus politics of pronoun, properties of language (arbitrariness of usage), semiotics, and linguistic features.

Extract 1: Interdiscursive Analysis

The interdiscursivity of extract 1 is partly projective and partly argumentative. This could be seen as the frame of reference of the entire document. The discourse in extract 1 has a claim to dialogue, but the language used was a classical example of mainstream Islamic *da'wa* (mission). It is an "open letter" and "call" to the Christians leaders to accept the Muslim concept of monotheism (Tawhid) and a "background" of Christian Trinity and the divinity of Christ. The "foregrounding" of Tawhid is "mainstream" in this phrase: *Between Us and You.*

In the Holy Qur'an, God Most High enjoins Muslims to issue the following call to Christians (and Jews—the People of the Scripture):

Say: O People of the Scripture! Come to a common word between us and you: that we shall worship none but God, and that we shall ascribe no partner unto Him, and that none of us shall take others for lords beside God. And if they turn away, then say: Bear witness that we are they who have surrendered (unto Him). (*Al-'Imran 3:64*) [par. 10]

The words: we shall ascribe no partner unto Him relate to the Unity of God, and the words: worship none but God, relate to being totally devoted to God. Hence they all relate to the First and Greatest Commandment. According to one of the oldest and most authoritative commentaries on the Holy Qur'an the words: that none of us shall take others for lords beside God, mean "that none of us should obey the other in disobedience to what God has commanded." This relates to the Second Commandment because justice and freedom of religion are a crucial part of love of the neighbour. [par. 11]

The preposition *between* signified in the proposition "*a common word*" seems to confine or restrict the command to us Muslims and you Christians or the other People of the Book). However, the *us* here could be viewed as object of *between*. In the beginning of paragraph 10 ("*In the Holy Qur'an, God Most High enjoins Muslims to issue the following call to Christians (and Jews—the People of the Scripture)*"), the emphasis that "God Most High 'enjoins' (ordered, commanded) Muslims (and not the Prophet himself) to issue the following call to Christians (and Jews—the *People of the Scripture*)" indicates that God values the Islamic monotheism more than that of Christianity and Judaism. It identifies that the idea of One God is fully and primarily complete in Islam than in other religions. This is one of the issues of claims to orthodoxy of which this book is arguing against because it seems to block moves to authentic communication between Muslims and Christians.

The pronouns *us* and *you* linked and/or separated by a conjunction *and* do not suggest that *us Muslims* and *you Christians* have a common understanding of the concept of God. Thus, the *and* is not "additive" contextually; rather, it suggests "difference" that makes the *us* to seemingly be in opposition to the *you*. Because *you* would have had *between* as its object, but it was separated by the conjunction *and*. The conjunction *and* maintains van Dijk's "ideological squares"—that is, "positive self-presentation and a simultaneous negative other-presentation" (quoted in Richardson 2007, p. 51). Paragraph 9 is typically an emphasis on the orthodoxy of Tawhid. It quotes the Qur'an and uses the Bible New Testament to substantiate the Tawhidic claims.

> Of God's Unity, God says in the Holy Qur'an: Say: He is God, the One! / God, the Self-Sufficient Besought of all! (*Al-Ikhlas* 112:1-2). Of the necessity of love for God, God says in the Holy Qur'an: So invoke the Name of thy Lord and devote thyself to Him with a complete devotion (*Al-Muzzammil* 73:8). [par. 9]

> In the New Testament, Jesus Christ . . . said: "Hear, O Israel, the Lord our God, the Lord is One. / And you shall love the Lord your God with all your heart, with all your soul, with all your mind, and with all your strength." This is the first commandment . . . (*Mk. 12:29-31*) [par. 9]

The idea of love of God in Islam is summarized in the *Shahadah*:

> The central creed of Islam consists of the two testimonies of faith or Shahadahs (i), which state that: There is no god but God, Muhammad is the messenger of God. These Two Testimonies are the sine qua non of Islam. He or she who testifies to them is a Muslim; he or she who denies them is not a Muslim. Moreover, the Prophet Muhammad . . . said: The best remembrance is: "There is no god but God" . . . .[ii] [par. 15]

Expanding on the best remembrance, the Prophet Muhammad . . . also said: The best that I have said—myself, and the prophets that came before me—is: "There is no god but God, He Alone, He hath no associate, His is the sovereignty and His is the praise and He hath power over all things" (iii). The phrases which follow the First Testimony of faith are all from the Holy Qur'an; each describes a mode of love of God, and devotion to Him. [par. 16]

The words: He Alone, remind Muslims that their hearts (iv) must be devoted to God Alone, since God says in the Holy Qur'an: God hath not assigned unto any man two hearts within his body (Al-Ahzab 33:4). God is Absolute and therefore devotion to Him must be totally sincere. [par. 17]

The words: He hath no associate, remind Muslims that they must love God uniquely, without rivals within their souls, since God says in the Holy Qur'an: Yet there are men who take rivals unto God: they love them as they should love God. But those of faith are more intense in their love for God . . . (Al-Baqarah 2:165). Indeed, their flesh and their hearts soften unto the remembrance of God . . . (Al-Zumar 39:23). [par. 18]

The words: His is the sovereignty; remind Muslims that their minds or their understandings must be totally devoted to God, for the sovereignty is precisely everything in creation or existence and everything that the mind can know. And all is in God's Hand, since God says in the Holy Qur'an: Blessed is He in Whose Hand is the sovereignty, and, He is Able to do all things (Al-Mulk 67:1). [par. 19]

The document claims that it is sine qua non of Islam (submission to God). It can be said here that the above paragraphs maintain the exclusivity of *valuing* Tawhidic monotheism. Testifying to it means that one is a "Muslim," and to deny it makes one a "non-Muslim."

The order of discourse insists on the unity of God. There is no compromise. It does not entertain any idea of associating partners to God. As if to hide the tone of the "open letter" from being a public protestation, the famous *surah Al-Ikhlas* 112, only *ayats* 1 and 2 were quoted (paragraphs 9 and 34): *"Say: He is God, the One! / God, the Self-Sufficient Besought of all! (Al-Ikhlas 112:1-2)."* The missing verses include "He begets not, nor was He begotten. And there is none co-equal or comparable unto Him." The leaving out of verses 3 and 4 of the *Al-Ikhlas* 112 could be to defuse the idea that extract 1 does not intend to provoke the Christians as did the Papal Address at University of Regensburg. Interdiscursively, extract 1 maintains a seesaw movement between the Qur'an and the Bible and metaphorically uses Qur'anic *ayat* and biblical verses to substantiate its propositions (see paragraphs 15-56 in appendix A).

From above, ipso facto, the use of language portrayed elements of Tawhidic network of practice. The language use above showed exclusivity in terms of *valuing* and *identifying*. Extract 1, though it projects in the beginning the new idea of interfaith dialogue based on love of God and neighbor, shifts basis to a sustained argumentation of Tawhidic claim to orthodoxy.

Extract 1: Linguistic Analysis—*Whole-Text Language Organization*

The text sets out to point out the difference between Islam and Christianity and even locating the difference to larger society. Paragraph 1 reveals the metonymic aspects of the text in the dates 1428 AH and October 13, 2007:

On the Occasion of the Eid al-Fitr al-Mubarak 1428 A.H/ October 13th 2007 C.E., and on the One Year Anniversary of the Open Letter of 38 Muslim Scholars to H.H. Pope Benedict XVI

They are indications of social and power relations. It may be by accident that the arabic number 38 and roman figures *XVI* are juxtaposed. But they help to substantiate the problem of difference hinted above and the problem of power struggle. Moreover, the use of different date representations are viewed as symbolic architectures of the mind and are semantically interpretable as structured objects consisting of symbols (O'Halloran 2003, p. 36). Cooper (1996, p. 28) gave an example of this kind of symbolic modelling:

> The symbol "34," for example, has parts (the symbols "3" and "4"), and the meaning of "34" is a function of the meaning of "3" in the tens position and "4" in the units position. The arabic representation of numbers, then, is a structured, semantically interpretable representation.

The same way, the roman figures *XVI* could be said to have been implanted to signify a representation associated with Christianity. Thus, it depicts the construction of the text as a "structured, semantically interpretable representation."

Then paragraphs 2-7 (see appendix A) were constructed to be a representation of structure of Christian hierarchies placing the Roman Catholic pope on the list as number one. Then, there is a litany of titles (His Holiness, His All Holiness, His Beatitude, Most Reverend) and different sees, countries, and churches. Was the arrangement meant to represent "first among equals" or "one among equals" in Christianity? Was it a ridicule in the seeming division in the Christian controversies over the unity of God? Was the titling of each Christian religious leader a way of evoking some consciousness? (see Richardson 2007, p. 49). The central messages of the discourse come in paragraphs 8 and 10:

> Muslims and Christians together make up well over half of the world's population. Without peace and justice between these two religious communities, there can be no meaningful peace in the world. The future of the world depends on peace between Muslims and Christians. [par. 8]

There is a power relation in paragraph 8 that suggests a threat to world peace if Islam and Christianity continue to live at daggers' drawn. The tone of the text is personal. It is an argumentative text soliciting responses from readers. Everyone likes peace and would want to be described as peaceful. Islam itself is said to signify "peace" as well. So the collocation of the word *peace* in this paragraph goes to portray that religious ideology of peace that Islam claims for itself. Therefore, if *you* cannot submit to the unity of God, *you* can submit because *we* (the world) need peace.

Paragraph 10 presents the idea of One God as nondialogical.

> In the Holy Qur'an, God Most High enjoins Muslims to issue the following call to Christians (and Jews—the People of the Scripture):
>
> Say: O People of the Scripture! Come to a common word between us and you: that we shall worship none but God, and that we shall ascribe no partner unto Him, and that none of us shall take others for lords beside God. And if they turn away, then say: Bear witness that we are they who have surrendered (unto Him). (*Al-'Imran* 3:64) [par. 10]

Hence, the mood of "come to a common word between us and you" is very imperative. It is an order that undervalues other approaches to God. It is an order that challenges the Christians and Jews. The coordinate clauses following the call to "a common word between us and you" makes insignificant what the Qur'an has attributed to Christianity in *surah Al-Ikhlas* 112. It is an indirect remark on the Christian conception of Jesus as Son of God and, indeed, second person of the Trinity.

Intertextuality is easily noticed throughout the discourse. For example, in paragraph 9,

> In the New Testament, Jesus Christ . . . said: "Hear, O Israel, the Lord our God, the Lord is One. / And you shall love the Lord your God with all your heart, with all your soul, with all your mind, and with all your strength." This is the first commandment. / And the second, like it, is this: 'You shall love your neighbour as yourself.' There is no other commandment greater than these. (*Mark 12:29-31*) [par. 9]

Here, extract 1 presents Jesus Christ as emphasizing the unity of God and disclaiming for himself that he is God. Passive voice was used to refer to Jesus as quoting from the Old Testament (Deuteronomy 6:4-5) to support the evidence that the Christians should not associate partner to God.

As part of mainstream nature of the document, there are arbitrary use of some arabic calligraphies that form properties of the text. Paragraphs 9, 15, 16, 25, 26, 28, 32, 35, 37, 38, 39, 40, 43 (see appendix A) follow particular conventions of respect for Prophet Muhammad (peace be upon him [*pbuh*]) and Jesus. They add to the aspect of *valuing* of the language of the Qur'an. Again, between paragraphs 22 and 28, the symbol of crescent was sandwiched in three different spaces before paragraphs 23, 25, and 28. That is "idea-writing" (Yule 1993), which signifies "increasing," and also it could be viewed as "word-writing" (Yule 1993), that is, "crescent," maintaining a "balance of power" with the "cross." Moreover, paragraphs 30 and 42 were ended by the unicode known as arabic start of *Rub El Hizb* (*Rub*, which means "quarter," and *Hizb*, which also means "a group"), which is a dividing system in the Qur'an for easier recitation. And paragraphs 38 and 45 were ended by arabic five-pointed star, which is a punctuation mark different from an asterisk (Latin *asteriscum*, "little star"). Though both symbols are unicodes, they are at the same time "picture-writing" (Yule 1993). They are all ways of *representing* and constructing identity.

The highlighted section titles and subtitles in extract 1 (see appendix A) are used to draw the attention of the reader to key issues of the discourse. At the same time, the text organization is styled to present to the reader with those words that are Qur'anically or biblically revealed. These words were put in italics to differentiate them from the authors' own writings. The reason for this might be to tell the reader that they are what God has ordered *us* and *you* to do. It goes back to the genre of an "open letter." The words in italics tell the reader that these are affirmation of what true love of God and love of neighbor should be.

Extract 1: *Clause Combination*

There is not one single verb in paragraphs 1-7 (see appendix A). They are made up of single words and complex phrases. The paragraphs 1-7 consist of names that are not so common (Theodoros II, Alexy II, Pavle, Ilia II, Chrisostomos, Christodoulos, Sawa, Christoforos, Shenouda III, Karekin II, Mar Thoma Didymos I, Abune Paulos). These paragraphs were enumerative.

Apart from paragraphs 1-7, the entire text consists mainly of compound and complex sentences. Most of the sentences consist of coordinate clauses (paragraphs 10, 11, 14, 16, 19, 20, 21, 22, 23, 24, 25, 27, 28, 29, 30, 31, 32, 34, 36, 37, 38, 39, 40, 41, 44, 45, 46, 47, 49, 51, 52, 53, 54, 55, 56) (see appendix A), for example, link up with coordinating conjunctions like *but, and, or, nor.* Paragraphs 12 and 18 are complex sentences consisting of a main clause and a subordinate clause; however, the subordinate conjunction *thus* begins the sentence.

> Thus in obedience to the Holy Qur'an, we as Muslims invite Christians to come together with us on the basis of what is common to us, which is also what is most essential to our faith and practice: the Two Commandments of love. [par. 12]

The subordinate conjunction for paragraph 18 is *since*, which gives paragraph 18 the features of main clause and subordinate clause.

> The words: He hath no associate, remind Muslims that they must love God uniquely, without rivals within their souls, since God says in the Holy Qur'an: [par. 18]

The reason for the complexity and compound nature of the text is that it is meant to be argumentative, citing pages of the Qur'an and the Bible to buttress the claim to unity of God based on Tawhidic principles and trying to create a wide gap between Tawhidic and Trinitarian monotheism as paragraphs 9-39 show (see appendix A). The syntax is mainly hypotactic and with a few clauses (for example, paragraph 11, "The words: we shall ascribe no partner unto Him relate to the Unity of God, and the words: worship none but God, relate to being totally devoted to God"). The use of conjunctions *and, but, or, nor, since,* for example, help to establish the argumentative nature of the text in trying to sustain the ideology of Tawhid.

Extract 1: *Clauses*

The mood of the text is *wholesomely* designated as imperative. The entire text is full of clauses that begin with a verb, *ordering* or *commanding* or even *requesting* Muslims, Christians, or Christians and Jews to action. Paragraph 9 line 7 (*Say*), paragraph 10 line 3 (*Say* and *Come*), paragraph 25 line 7 (*Say*), paragraph 26 line 4 (*Say*), paragraph 31 line 2 (*Hear*), paragraph 53 line 4 (*Say*) are just examples of imperative mood:

> Of God's Unity, God says in the Holy Qur'an: Say: He is God, the One! / God, the Self-Sufficient Besought of all! (*Al-Ikhlas 112: 1-2*) [par.9]

> Say: O People of the Scripture! Come to a common word between us and you: [par. 10]
> Say: Lo! my worship and my sacrifice and my living and my dying are for God, Lord of the Worlds. / He hath no partner. [par. 25]

> Say, (O Muhammad, to mankind): If ye love God, follow me; [par. 26]

> The Shema in the Book of Deuteronomy (6: 4-5), a centerpiece of the Old Testament and of Jewish liturgy, says: Hear, O Israel: The LORD our God, the LORD is one! [par. 31]

> God says in the Holy Qur'an: Say (O Muslims): We believe in God and that which is revealed unto us [par. 53]

Such imperative moods go to sustain the argumentation of claim to orthodoxy in regard to unity of God. It makes a common word a document that has been streamlined to follow the underpinnings of divine revelation infused in the Qur'an. The lexemes of the text reveal various morphemes that have been used in the construction of the document. For example, paragraph 8 (*world's* and *world*); paragraphs 8, 9, 10 (*Christians* and *Christianity*); paragraphs 9, 11, 12 (*commandment, commandments,* and *command*).

As part of the discursivity of the text, in its bid to maintain the dichotomy between *us Muslims* and *you Christians*, it reveals synonyms in terms that are not shared by all. For example, when the Qur'an says the People of the Scripture, its emphasis is usually on the Christians and Jews because of the Holy Bible and the Torah. Here, in this context, Qur'an is synonymous with the Bible. However, the construction of the text shows a strong demarcation between the two sacred books. The appellation "Holy" is given to the Qur'an (Holy Qur'an), but none was given to the Bible. The Qur'an was considered as Holy Qur'an in these paragraphs: 9, 10, 11, 12, 16, 19, 20, 21, 22, 24, 25, 26, 27, 30, 41, 47, 48, 49, 51, 52, 53, 55, 56 (see appendix A). But there is no place in the text where the Bible is called holy. That goes back to the argument that the Qur'an is an eternal word of God, divinely revealed to Prophet Muhammad, while the Bible was inspired and at the same time it has been corrupted by Christians. This idea can be contrasted in paragraph 9: "Of God's Unity, God says in the Holy Qur'an." The use of active voice here makes God's presence in the Qur'an evident and the Qur'an can be interpreted as Holy and eternal. Whereas in paragraph 39 "the Prophet Muhammad . . . was perhaps, through inspiration, restating and alluding to the biblical First Commandment." Here, Prophet Muhammad was depicted as "perhaps" interpreting or restating or alluding to the *Shema* of Deuteronomy 6:4-5. God does not speak when reference to the Bible was made in paragraph 39. Rather, it was Prophet Muhammad's inspiration and interpretation, not God's. Thus, the term *Holy* as used in the text signifies "*valuing.*" While the Holy Qur'an is valued so much, the Bible (that has been corrupted by Christians) is not valued.

The discourse—a common word between us and you—continues to reiterate the problem of difference between *us Muslims* and *you Christians.* Between paragraphs 14 and 15, the subtitle says, "Love of God in *Islam,*" and before paragraph 40, another subtitle says, "Love of the neighbor in *Islam.*" These subtitles are to be contrasted with "Love of God as the first and greatest commandment in the *Bible*" (between paragraphs 30 and 31) and "Love of the neighbor in the *Bible*" (between paragraphs 42 and 43). The difference here is that Muslims' basis for love of God and love of the neighbor is rooted in religion (Islam) while the Christians' basis for love of God and love of the neighbor is rooted in the scripture (Bible).

The connotation here is that love of God and neighbor cannot be imagined in Christianity because some Muslim scholars (Bawany 1977, Rahim 2003) believed that Christianity was founded by St. Paul and not Jesus Christ. So love of God and neighbor should rather be rooted to the Bible. On the other hand, Muslims believe that Islam, as a religion, is *din al-fitrah*, Abrahamic and primordial (see Joseph Nnabugwu, Dissertation: *Discourse Analytical Investigation of the Paradigms of Trinitarianism and Tawhidism in Christian-Muslim Relations* [University of Aberdeen, 2010]).

Extract 1: *Words*

The words used in the text were carefully selected. First, to promote the idea of the unity of God. Second, to portray the dialectics of the document. Paragraph 9 ("foundational principles of both faiths") sets off the dialectic trope. But most of the time, the dialectics are swallowed by the Tawhidic principles of monotheism (see appendix A, paragraphs 15-29).

Inasmuch as the document is constructed to be argumentative, the modal features suggest some categorical imperatives that are meant to be binding to both Christians and Muslims. For example, paragraphs 9, 10, and 11 used the "modal prediction/intention" of *shall* to insist on the unity of God.

> And you *shall* (italics mine) love the Lord your God with all your heart, with all your soul, with all your mind, and with all your strength. [par. 9]

> That we *shall* (italics mine) worship none but God, and that we *shall* (italics mine) ascribe no partner unto Him, and that none of us *shall* (italics mine) take others for lords beside God. [par. 10]

> The words: we *shall* (italics mine) ascribe no partner unto Him relate to the Unity of God, and the words [par. 11]

Paragraphs 17, 19, 20, 21, 23, and 25 (see appendix A) used the "modal control" of *must* to insist on the nondialogical nature of the oneness of God. Paragraph 11 ("*That none of us* (should) [emphasis mine] *obey the other in disobedience to what God has commanded*") and paragraph 18 ("*Yet there are men who take rivals unto God: they love them as they* (should) [emphasis mine] *love God*") used the "modal obligation" of *should* to argue for nonsubmissiveness to anybody or thing but God alone.

Paragraph 20 ("*It thus ends with prayers for grace and guidance, so that we* (might) [emphasis mine] *attain—through what begins with praise and gratitude—salvation and love*") and paragraph 22 ("*If ye go not forth He* (will) [emphasis mine] *afflict you with a painful doom, and* (will) [emphasis mine] *choose instead of you a folk other than you*") used the "modal reassurance/possibility" of *might* and *will*. The modal features used and the imperative mood of the text make its dialectics a subsumption that is nondialogical. This is another way of *representing* the document. The foregoing reveals the example of how Muslims construct themselves in Tawhidic ideology. By this, they tend to "foreground" Tawhid and "background" any trace of the Trinity. Now, extract 2 will be analyzed so as to bring out also the way Christians "foreground" the idea of the Trinity.

Chapter Five

Loving God and Neighbor Together

The Christian response to the Muslim leaders' "open letter and call" is a discourse by which its semiotic is influenced. The Christian response, referred to here as extract 2, is partly a responsive and partly a rejoinder. Analyzing extract 2 and in like manner of extract 1, Fairclough's framework—interactional analysis, interdiscursive analysis, linguistic analysis (examining the whole-text organization), clause combination, clauses, and words—will be applied.

Extract 2, titled in jumbo, "Loving God and Neighbor Together: A Christian Response to *A Common Word Between Us and You*"[5] is a discourse whose semiotic is derived from the discourse of extract 1. The discourse of extract 2 (see appendix B) sounds partly a "responsive" and partly a "rejoinder." At first glance, it seems that extract 2 was a reaction to the interfaith initiative. It does show that the Christians have their wits about a common word. Extract 1 emphasized that the foundational principles of both faiths are "love of God and love of the neighbor." The lexeme *love* has one morpheme, and at the same time, it is used as a noun. But the Christians titled theirs as "Loving God and

Neighbor Together." The lexeme *loving* has two morphemes (lov-ing). It can be interpreted both as a verb and an adjective. The context used above was verbal, which is nominalizing. In the phrase *loving God and neighbor together*, the agent is remotely removed from it. Otherwise, it would have read "*We* love God and Neighbor Together." Instead, it says, "*Loving* God and Neighbor Together," and then, it adds "A Christian Response to *A Common Word Between Us and You*." Its interpretation could read, "*We Love* God and Neighbor, this is a Christian Response to *A Common Word Between Us and You*." At the title level, the discourse could be seen as declarative. But the Christians did not want to claim outright that they love God and their neighbor. There are other elements involved in the network practices of extract 2.

The Christian response could be viewed as a retort because of the publicity a common word was given by the originators. The introductory words to the text indicated that the Christian response has been advertised twice in the tabloid *New York Times* (October 13, 2007 and November 18, 2007). Again, the response of the Christians was noted to have been drafted by scholars at Yale Divinity School's Centre for Faith and Culture, signed by, first, four signatories and endorsed by almost three hundred Christian theologians and leaders. This brings out the rivalry in the discourses of Islam and Christianity. "A common word between us and you," the Muslims' initiative document, was institutionally maintained by the Royal Aal al-Bayt Institute for Islamic Thought, Jordan; the Christian response was equally institutionally constructed by scholars at Yale Divinity School's Centre for Faith and Culture.

Summary of Extract 2: Interactional Analysis

Extract 2 consists of sixteen paragraphs identified by this book for quick reference. Paragraphs 1 and 2 refer to the reason why the text was written. The text indicated that it was a response to an "open letter" sent by "Muslim scholars and clerics (October 13, 2007) to leaders of Christian churches, everywhere" (see ACWWP 2008). The Christian response did not observe the 1428 AH date as used in extract 1. Perhaps the reason for such pronounced oversight might be, as it claimed, "to promote constructive engagement between these major religious communities" (par. 2). Further in paragraph 3 it claims that: "Jesus Christ's call to love God and neighbor was rooted in the divine revelation to the people of Israel embodied in the Torah" (Deuteronomy 6:5, Leviticus 19:18). Further in paragraph 4 it asserts that: "Since Jesus Christ says, "First take the log out your own eye, and then you will see clearly to take the speck out of your neighbor's eye" (Matthew 7:5); this can be seen as a leitmotif. (see appendix B). Emphasis is on "Jesus Christ" (with Trinitarian understanding) as the second person of the Trinity (that is, Jesus Christ equal in majesty with God the Father: True God from True God) and messiah. It heralds Jesus Christ's call to love of God and neighbor. In paragraph 4, the Christians sound remorseful as they ask forgiveness of God and the Muslim community for the Crusades and the excesses of the war on terror. The intertextuality here is in part an imitation of the publicity the text was given in extract 1. And in another instance, it sounds like a frame of reference for Christians' claim to "constructive engagement." Terms like *forgiveness* and *reconciliation* are so much associated with faith-based diplomacy, hence the importance of the term *drafted* as used in paragraph 2.

Paragraph 5 has a subtitle indicating "religious peace" - "world peace." The "hyphenation" of *religious peace* to *world peace* revisits the argument in extract 1 about the importance of peace between Christians and Muslims.

Paragraph 6 described and ensconced (established comfortably) on the phrase *common "ground"* instead of *common "word."* The *ground* here signifies the subject of debate. The common "ground" cannot be what the Qur'an designated as "a common *word* between us and you: that we shall worship none but God, and that we shall ascribe no partner unto Him" (*Al-'Imran* 3:64). The idea of "word" and the command "that we shall ascribe no partner unto Him" could be viewed as a provocation of Trinitarian ideology.

Paragraphs 7, 8, and 9 applaud the initiative of "a common word between us and you" and stress its emphasis on the love of God as central to "every believer." The metonym "every believer" sounds all-inclusive. It does not raise the problem of difference. This goes back to inform the reader of the title of this discourse: "Loving God and Neighbor *Together*." *Together* here suggests collectivity.

Paragraphs 10, 11, 12, and 13 present love of neighbor as a necessary condition to claim love of God. The text also remarked that if there is no justice, love of God and neighbor can never exist.

Paragraphs 14, 15, and 16 seek to promote the cause love of God and neighbor as a task and, at the same time, "the basis of all future interfaith dialogue between Christians and Muslims." The text argues conclusively that peace between the two religious communities is important; otherwise, the text refers to extract 1 here, "our eternal souls are at stake as well."

Extract 2: Interdiscursive Analysis

The Christian response could be viewed as a "responsive" and/or a "rejoinder." It can be viewed as declarative of convictions. Though the discourse is not as long as extract 1, it concisely says what it wants to say. It claims ab initio that its aim is to "promote constructive engagement between these major religious communities" (paragraph 2). It never said "between *us* and *you*"; rather, it used a metonym (these major religious communities) replacing Islam and Christianity. The choice of such metonym does not raise so much problem of difference. Is it "drafted" (paragraph 2) as one of its plan to promote constructive engagement, or is it part of the promotional nature of the text? Indeed, it claims to conduct some major conferences and workshops (paragraph 2). The text has appeared twice as an advertisement in *The New York Times* (October 13 and November 18, 2007). Such media attention might be viewed as trying to have equal leverage with the discourse of extract 1. It argues that getting an "open letter" was a sign of a "Muslim hand of conviviality and cooperation" (paragraph 3).

The order of discourse was *ensconced* with carefully chosen terms. For example, the title "Loving God and Neighbor Together" presents the "adverbial modality" *together* as insisting on a cooperation and interchange between Muslims and Christians. The title can as well say, "Loving together." Because of the title, there is no place in the text, unless referring to the original document, "A Common Word Between Us and You"; it used between *us* and *you*. Rather, it used phrases such as "Christianity and Islam" (paragraph 3), "against our Muslim neighbor" (paragraph 4), "Muslims and Christians" (paragraph 5), "common between us" and "between our two communities" (paragraph 6).

The text explicitly "backgrounded" the Islamic calendar. Extract 1 (1428 AH) was "foregrounded" as counterbalancing the Gregorian calendar (October 13, 2007), which, of course, began with *anno Domini* (in the year of the Lord). However, the text "foregrounds" Jesus Christ (paragraphs 3, 4, 12).

> Jesus Christ's call to love God and neighbor was rooted in the divine revelation to the people of Israel embodied in the Torah (Deuteronomy 6:5; Leviticus 19:18). [par. 3]

> Since Jesus Christ says, "First take the log out your own eye, and then you will see clearly to take the speck out of your neighbor's eye" (Matthew 7:5). [par. 4]

> "But I say unto you," says Jesus Christ, "Love your enemies and pray for those who persecute you, so that you may be children of your Father in heaven; for he makes his sun rise on the evil and on the good" (Matthew 5: 44-45). Our love, Jesus Christ says,

> must imitate the love of the infinitely good Creator; our love must be as unconditional as is God's—extending to brothers, sisters, neighbors, and even enemies. At the end of his life, Jesus Christ himself prayed for his enemies: "Forgive them; for they do not know what they are doing" (Luke 23:34). [par. 12]

It presents Jesus Christ as the Christian model, teacher, life, way, and truth. The denotation here makes Christians apparently the followers of Jesus Christ. From here, the Christians construct their identity to be consistent with Christ's injunction: to love God and neighbor. The references to the Crusades and excesses of war on terror and asking forgiveness for them are parts of imitating Jesus Christ. This is *identifying* with Jesus Christ; *identifying* with the second person of the Trinity. This is "foregrounding" Trinitarian understanding of the Godhead.

The semiotics of the text seems to connect to the political networks of practices. The introduction of terminologies like *Crusades* and *war on terror* make Christianity a religion that sinned, and therefore, it needed to ask for forgiveness.

> Before we "shake your hand" in responding to your letter, we ask forgiveness of the All-Merciful One and of the Muslim community around the world. [par. 4]

Or did the text introduce the terminology *Crusades* in order to infer the presence of the symbol of the crescent in extract 1 (between paragraphs 22 and 23, 24 and 28)? To ask forgiveness for the two (Crusades and war on terror), Christian involvements might be seen as part of making public confession.

Extract 2: Linguistic Analysis—*Whole-Text Organization*

The discourse seems declarative. It was meant for a wider audience than being confined to Muslims and Christians. Its classification in the press was advertisement. This suggests that it was a hybrid. The genre is hybrid. It seeks "to promote constructive engagement" (paragraph 2) and, at the same time, underlines the task of interfaith dialogue between Muslims and Christians. It claims that this is its aim.

> "Let this common ground"—the dual common ground of love of God and of neighbor—"be the basis of all future interfaith dialogue between us," your courageous letter urges. [par. 14]

As mentioned above, the title reminds the reader the difference of approach to the Muslim call to *A Common Word Between Us and You*. The text simulated faith-based diplomacy of "forgiveness" and "reconciliation" (paragraph 4). Instead of arguing on the unity of God as the basis of common ground, the Christians' response was based on "cooperation between Christians and Muslims can be hallmark of the relations between the two communities" as noted in paragraph 6. Generally, the entire discourse sounds like a reaction to extract 1.

Extract 2: *Clause Combination*

The text consists of simple, compound, and complex sentences. The opening sentence (paragraph 1) is a simple sentence consisting of a single clause.

> On October 13, 2007, on the occasion of Eid al-Fitr, 138 Muslim scholars and clerics sent an open letter "to leaders of Christian churches, everywhere." [par.1]

The second sentence is a compound.

> The signatories to that letter, titled A Common Word Between Us and You, include top leaders from around the world representing every major school of Islamic thought. [par. 1]

The syntax is paratactic (that is, the clauses in the sentence were introduced without any conjunctions).

In paragraph 3, the second sentence is very complex.

> A Common Word Between Us and You identifies some core common ground between Christianity and Islam which lies at the heart of our respective faiths as well as at the heart of the most ancient Abrahamic faith, Judaism. [par. 3]

The syntax is hypotactic. There were uses of conjunctions like *as well as*. The complexity of the fifth sentence of paragraph 3 is an argument that sustains conviviality in seeking to love God and neighbor.

> In this response we extend our own Christian hand in return, so that together with all other human beings we may live in peace and justice as we seek to love God and our neighbors.

It is very explicit in the text that there is a need for genuine Muslim-Christian relations, hence, the indirect way of Christian suggestion of ways of resolving conflicts—that is, by "asking for forgiveness and seeking for reconciliation" as observed in paragraph 4. For this authentic communication to happen, the Christians offered to step forward to ask for forgiveness. The metaphoric expression in repeating Jesus Christ's command, the Christians formed a chain of complex discourse that shows both paratactic and hypotactic syntaxes.

> Muslims and Christians have not always shaken hands in friendship; their relations have sometimes been tense, even characterized by outright hostility. Since Jesus Christ says, "First take the log out your own eye, and then you will see clearly to take the speck out of your neighbor's eye" (Matthew 7:5), we want to begin by acknowledging that in the past (e.g., in the Crusades) and in the present (e.g., in excesses of the "war on terror") many Christians have been guilty of sinning against our Muslim neighbors. Before we "shake your hand" in responding to your letter, we ask forgiveness of the All-Merciful One and of the Muslim community around the world. [par. 4]

The arguments in the text are built in as reactions to the claims in extract 1. There was nothing new (except the "foreground" of the Christian understanding of forgiveness and reconciliation that is based on Jesus Christ's command to love your enemies and pray for those who persecute you). It is clear from extract 2 that more often Jesus Christ is mentioned than God the Father.

> As Christians we resonate deeply with this sentiment. Our faith teaches that we must be with our neighbors—indeed, that we must act in their favor—even when our neighbors turn out to be our enemies. "But I say unto you," says Jesus Christ, "Love your enemies and pray for those who persecute you, so that you may be children of your Father in heaven; for he makes his sun rise on the evil and on the good" (Matthew 5:44-45). [par. 12]

Other information in the text are rejoinders. As part of that reaction to extract 1, paragraph 15 hinted that love of God in Islam is based on the *Shahadahs* and they are sine qua non of Islam. But the Christian response was categorically linked with the modal control *must*: "Our love Jesus Christ says, *must* (italics mine) imitate the love of the infinitely good Creator; our love must be as unconditional as is God's—extending to brothers, sisters, neighbors, and even enemies" (paragraph 12). While Muslims argue that the condition for love of God in Islam is profession of the *Shahadah*, the Christians maintained that love of God has no conditions.

> Our love, Jesus Christ says, must imitate the love of the infinitely good Creator; our love must be as unconditional as is God's—extending to brothers, sisters, neighbors, and even enemies. At the end of his life, Jesus Christ himself prayed for his enemies: "Forgive them; for they do not know what they are doing" (Luke 23:34). [par.12]

The Christians are here constructing a representation of multiculturality of humanity that implicitly is *representing* the unity in the Trinity.

Extract 2: *Clauses*

The clauses are mostly indicative (that is, denoting moods of verbs used in the arguments that tend to suggest something). It is a way of maintaining the responsiveness of the discourse to interfaith initiative. The indicative moods could be observed in "were deeply" (paragraph 3), "shake your hands" (paragraph 4, last sentence). In the same paragraph 4, first sentence, "shaken hands in friendship" designates another mood (subjunctive). It is subjunctive because Muslims and Christians have been suspicious of themselves. So the past participle verb *shaken* signifies the mood of subjunctive.

The modalities of these indicative and subjunctive clauses are articulated to fit into the argumentation of the discourse. The way the modal reassurance of *may* was used in paragraph 3, last sentence ("we *may* live in peace" [italics mine]), is characteristic of the indicative mood of the discourse. Paragraphs 4

("First take the log out your own eye, and then you *will* [italics mine]see clearly to take the speck out of your neighbor's eye") and 5 ("If we can achieve religious peace between these two religious communities, peace in the world *will* [italics mine] clearly be easier to attain") used the modal possibility of *will* to engage on the inevitability of peace; the modal control of *can* and *must* (paragraphs 5 and 12) insist on the obligation of being with one's neighbors.

> Without peace and justice between these two religious communities, there *can* (italics mine) be no meaningful peace in the world. [par. 5]

> Our faith teaches that we *must* (italics mine) be with our neighbors—indeed, that we *must* (italics mine) act in their favor—even when our neighbors turn out to be our enemies. [par. 12]

Then, paragraph 10 used the modal negative (*cannot*) to insist on the condition that loving God means, first of all, to love the neighbor whom one sees before loving God.

> In the New Testament we similarly read, "whoever does not love [the neighbor] does not know God" (I John 4:8) and "whoever does not love his brother whom he has seen *cannot* (italics mine) love God whom he has not seen" (I John 4:20). [par. 10]

To maintain the "loving . . . together" claim of the text, the discourse made use of pronouns that only convoke both Muslims and Christians together. It did not use much of the "ideological squares" (van Dijk) between *Us Muslims and You Christians*. The prevalent pronouns in this text are *we*, *us*, *our*. There are variations in the use of *we* in this context. The first usage of *we* (paragraph 3) represents the Christian scholars and theologians. The second usage of *we* (paragraph 3, last sentence) refers to Muslims. So are the uses of *us* and *our*. Generally, it might be argued that Christian scholars presented their discourse suggesting (through the indicative and subjunctive moods) a "constructive engagement" that could be based on forgiveness and reconciliation. However, in the very last sentence, the discourse squares up *we* (representing the Christians) and *you* (representing the Muslims) in affirmation that they are committed to "labor together in heart, soul, mind, and strength" (paragraph 16).

Extract 2: *Words*

A very distinctive word throughout the discourse is the replacement of *common* "*word*" with *common* "*ground*" (paragraph 6). The reason was mentioned above. The construction of the text presents some antonyms together (*friendship* and *hostility*) (paragraph 4) and, in some other places, synonyms (*conviviality* and *cooperation*) (paragraph 3). This is part of the indicative mood of the discourse. It is always making suggestions and plans for "future interfaith dialogue" between Muslims and Christians. Unlike in extract 1, where there were grand etymological definitions of *heart, soul, mind, will,* and *strength*, extract 2 just evoked strong sentiments of *soul, heart, mind, strength,* seeking only to know how God would use them as instruments of love and peace.

The two extracts 1 and 2 have different interdiscursivity and text organization. The former's mood is imperative. It purposefully sustained an argumentation that "foregrounds" Tawhid. The latter, its mood is indicative and partly subjunctive. It is also a declaration. It developed such approach because it claims "to promote constructive engagement." The text "backgrounds" the hyperbolic exposition of unity of God while at the same time utilizing the construct of the Trinity in its "draft" for forgiveness and reconciliation. Below, therefore, this study will examine the different approaches of the texts (extracts 1 and 2) and from the White Paper and other extracts (3, 4, 5, 6, 7, 8, 9) to see how they can be applied to building authentic communication between Muslims and Christians.

Chapter Six

Ways to Authentic Communication

Ways of authentic communication between Muslims and Christians are possible if both religious communities can evolve an interfaith initiative that acknowledges equality, differences, otherness, and diversity. It is not the scope of this book to delve into theories or philosophies of authenticity or communication. In this book a common word project is viewed as Muslim-Christian "public sphere" or "meeting point." It is the basis of suggested ways to authentic communication in Muslim-Christian relations. In the two extracts analyzed above, there are conscious efforts and moves toward the possibility for authentic communication, hence the reason for the interfaith initiative and collation of articles that made up *A Common Word 'White Paper' Booklet 2008*. The identity constructions, dichotomies, and demarcations created in the construction of the texts, though substantive, may not undermine the "meeting-point-ness" or the "public sphere-ness" of the "call" to a common word.

A common word could be viewed as a "public sphere" (Fairclough 1999, Habermas 1989, Warren 1995) between Muslims and Christians. It could serve as converging and diverging points for liberating actions and discourses between Muslims and Christians. A particular aspect of a common word that observes the presence of the other is the recognition of the difference between *us Muslims* and *you Christians*. This is a way forward to authentic communication. A common word is a "public sphere" that debates on differences and similarities between Islam and Christianity and yet in its inception, it finds it difficult not to make one belief system a *be-all* and *end-all* of orthodoxy.

Authentic communication can only come into place when various issues raised in the course of analyzing extracts 1 and 2 are tackled. The primary issue is the problem of orthodoxy claims that is based on the concept of monotheism. Shall a common word be based exclusively on the love of God, especially as entrenched in the concepts of monotheism? Or shall a common word be practical enough in horizontal relations of love of neighbor and then proceed to the vertical relations of love of God? The divide in the terminologies—a common *word* or a common *ground*—add more to the problem of difference or representation associated with the claims to orthodoxy. What is the mood of the discourse? Should it remain imperative as initiated in extract 1, or should the mood change to indicative mood as the verbs usages suggest? Should the arguments between Islam and Christianity be sustained by "foregrounding" the differences and "backgrounding" the similarities or vice versa? In this stage 4, there is a need to look for ways past the obstacles mentioned above.

Different genres that add up to the formation of the White Paper portray that since the beginning of the interfaith initiative of a common word, so many conferences, resolutions, interviews, addresses, final statements, press releases, seminars, workshops, fora, and speeches have been held and conducted. These events have tried to emphasize the importance of interrelations between the

Muslim and Christian individuals. Basically, they tend to promote various ways of making practical the loving of neighbor. Let us now examine the genres and the discourses of these resolutions with particular emphases on the final statements, final declarations, communiqué, and speeches of which both Muslims and Christians jointly constructed in order to see how they make propositions for authentic communication between themselves.

**White Paper: Conferences, Documents, and Resolutions—
Yale Workshop and Conference**

The workshop and conference (24-31 July 2008) titled *Loving God and Neighbor in Word and Deed: Implications for Christians and Muslims* was convened by the Yale Center for Faith and Culture in collaboration with the Royal *Aal Al-Bayt* Institute and was held at Yale University, USA. This included both a scholarly workshop and a broader conference. The workshop and conference attracted over 120 leading Muslim and Christian leaders and scholars. These resolutions were summarized in a four-point-count final statement issued at the end of the Yale Conference. Extract 3 below shows, among other things, that they agreed on the following:

Extract 3: Yale Conference's Four-Point-Count Final Statement

1. Muslims and Christians affirm the unity and absoluteness of God. We recognize that God's merciful love is infinite, eternal and embraces all things. This love is central to both our religions and is at the heart of the Judeo-Christian-Islamic monotheistic heritage.
2. We recognize that all human beings have the right to the preservation of life, religion, property, intellect, and dignity. No Muslim or Christian should deny the other these rights, nor should they tolerate

the denigration or desecration of one another's sacred symbols, founding figures, or places of worship.

3. We are committed to these principles and to furthering them through continuous dialogue. We thank God for bringing us together in this historic endeavor and ask that He purify our intentions and grant us success through His all-encompassing Mercy and Love.

4. We Christian and Muslim participants meeting together at Yale for the historic A Common Word conference denounce and deplore threats made against those who engage in interfaith dialogue. Dialogue is not a departure from faith; it is a legitimate means of expression and an essential tool in the quest for the common good. (see ACWWP 2008)

The joint discourse of Muslims and Christians gave vent to their common agreement upon the unity and absoluteness of God, but it has to be in accordance with the specificity of the individual religion's monotheistic heritage. Here the word *heritage* refers to something handed down by tradition, something that can be said to be inalienably the people's belonging.

The second statement made a good choice of the word *recognition* as a way of respecting, among other things, the "religion" of the other. Here, the problematics of difference was raised, but at the same time, the acceptance that the other's religion should be given recognition and not "misrecognition" or "nonrecognition" (Taylor 1992) is a way forward to authentic communication. The workshop and conference claimed to be committed to statements 1 and 2 and, at the same time, declared that those should be objects of the Muslim-Christian dialogue.

White Paper: Cambridge Conference

The Cambridge University and Lambeth Palace, UK, organized a conference (12-15 October 2008). The White Paper claims that on the occasion of the anniversary of the issuing of A Common Word Between Us and You, a conference titled 'A Common Word and Future Muslim-Christian Engagement,' was hosted by the Archbishop of Canterbury in collaboration with the University of Cambridge Inter-Faith Programme and the Royal *Aal Al-Bayt* Institute and held at the University of Cambridge with a final session at Lambeth Palace. The conference came out with a communiqué. The conference claims to commit itself for the following year these tasks:

Extract 4: Cambridge Conference's Communiqué

The communiqué of the Cambridge and Lambeth Palace conference simulates the semiotic of public domain observed above in extracts 1 and 2. The communiqué emphasizes the following:

1. To identify and promote the use of educational materials, for all age-groups and in the widest possible range of languages, that we accept as providing a fair reflection of our faiths
2. To build a network of academic institutions, linking scholars, students and academic resources, with various committees and teams which can work on shared values
3. To identify funds to facilitate exchanges between those training for roles of leadership within our religious communities
4. To translate significant texts from our two traditions for the use of the other. (see ACWWP 2008)

The conference claims by its public announcement of their deliberation that "education of all age-groups in the widest possible range of languages" is a genuine means of understanding one another, especially in matters of faith. The conference also argues that knowledge transfer through student and institution exchanges could be vehicles of bridging the gaps posed by the problematic of difference. It further proposes that translation of significant texts from the two traditions of Islam and Christianity for the use of *other* is of paramount importance. The *other* here signifies not "sameness" or "identity." Rather, it signifies "alterity." The translation of these significant texts will help the "other" understand another as they interact in matters of faith and in the dialogues, especially about the concepts of monotheism.

White Paper: Catholic-Muslim Forum

The "First Seminar of the Catholic-Muslim Forum (4-6 November 2008)" was held in Rome and organized by the Pontifical Council for Interreligious Dialogue in collaboration with the Royal *Aal Al-Bayt* Institute in Amman. The agenda of the conference included discussion of the spiritual and theological fundamentals of Islam and Christianity, the need for human dignity and mutual respect, an audience with Pope Benedict XVI, and addresses by Sheikh Mustafa Ceric (the grand mufti of Bosnia Herzegovina) and Professor Seyyed Hossein Nasr. The conference also produced a declaration. The interest of this book is on the declaration of the conference. In the final declaration of the conference, they drew out points of similarity and of diversity that reflect the distinctive specific genius of the two religions. Below is an analysis of the Catholic-Muslim final declaration.[6] It is a fifteen-point-count declaration.

Extract 5: Catholic-Muslim Forum's Final Declaration

The main focus of the final declaration establishes the Christian belief in the nature of Jesus as the Son of God and extols at the same time the Trinitarian concept of God. It also maintains the Christian conception of God as Father and Jesus as Son. Hence, point 1 says,

For Christians the source and example of love of God and neighbor is the love of Christ for his Father, for humanity and for each person. God is Love (I Jn 4:16) and "God so loved the world that He gave his only Son so that whoever believes in him shall not perish but have eternal life" (Jn 3:16). God's love is placed in the human heart through the Holy Spirit.

Again, it establishes Islamic understanding of God as one and indivisible unity. The same point 1 says,

Love is a timeless transcendent power which guides and transforms human mutual regard. This love, as indicated by the Holy and Beloved Prophet Muhammad, is prior to the human love for the One True God. A Hadith indicates that God's loving compassion for humanity is even greater than that of a mother for her child (*Muslim, Bab al Tawba*: 21).

It observes here that the representatives and theologians of these two communities, through this declaration, have agreed to disagree, especially in matters about the nature of God and Jesus. For the Christians, it is the Trinity and Jesus is the Son of God, while for Muslims, it is Tawhid and Jesus cannot be associated to God. Generally, the conference emphasized the importance of the fundamental human rights given to all persons by God. They maintained that these rights should in no way be undermined by anybody or institution. That's the signification of points 2-6 (See appendix C).

Point 10 emphasizes the need for both Islam and Christianity to provide education that is very sincere and genuine in teaching the young people about the religious values of the "other" as this will lead to further and proper understanding and openness.

> We are convinced that Catholics and Muslims have the duty to provide a sound education in human, civic, religious and moral values for their respective members and to promote accurate information about each other's religions.

This book, however, notices the change of the use of pronoun here to mean collectivity and a signification of unity of purpose. For example, *We affirm* (italics mine) (points 4 and 8), *we recognize* (italics mine) (point 9), *we are convinced* (italics mine) (point 10), *we profess* (italics mine) (point 11), *we call* (italics mine) (point 12), *we have agreed* (italics mine) (point 14), *we look forward* (italics mine) (point 15) (see appendix C). Inasmuch as they maintained their different religious stands, but for authentic communication to be achievable, they dropped the politics of pronoun that is divisional and adopted the pronoun that is all-inclusive.

White Paper: Eugen Biser Award Ceremony

Included in the White Paper a genre of "award ceremony" was the Eugen Biser Award, which was conferred to "A Common Word Between Us and You" on November 2, 2008. The recipients of the award were HRH Prince Ghazi bin Muhammad, Sheikh Al-Habib Ali Al-Jifri, and Reisu-l-Ulema Dr. Mustafa Ceric. The reason for the Eugen Biser Award in Munich, Germany, was to acknowledge the contributions of the recipients to Muslim-Christian dialogue.

At the award ceremony, Prince Ghazi gave a speech, and his speech was an articulation of the reason for a common word. His speech was comprised of three parts. Part 1 was a review of one year of a common word; part 2 was the theological motives behind the formation of a common word. Among other things, the issues he raised in particular that necessitated a common word were the mistakes in the Papal Address at the University of Regensburg (September 2006) and the need for peace between Muslims and Christians. Part 3 dealt with the expectations from a common word. This book has a fascination for his analogy of a *butum* tree. According to him, under that tree the idea of a common word was hatched.

Extract 6: Eugen Biser Award Ceremony Speech—Prince Ghazi bin Muhammad (1)

> For in September 2007, one month before the launch of A Common Word, I had the privilege to visit this tree twice, once in the company of a number of the scholars behind the Common Word initiative (including Shaykh Habib Ali, who is here today), and it was under this tree that we prayed to God (or at least I did) to grant A Common Word success. (see ACWWP 2008)

The reason for such interest or fascination is that there is a kind of link between Prince Ghazi's *butum* tree analogy to the fundamental bases: love of God and love of neighbor of a common word between us Muslims and you Christians. He described the age of the *butum* tree, its estranged location in the desert, and its height. He clearly stated that the *butum* tree was a kind of *pistachio* tree as noted in extract 7:

Extract 7: Eugen Biser Award Ceremony Speech—Prince Ghazi bin Muhammad (2)

> In the middle of the eastern Jordanian desert, in a place called Safawi, miles away from anything, from any landmark or any human traces, there stands a unique, solitary tree. This tree is around 1500 years old and there are no other trees to be seen for dozens of miles

> in any direction. Despite its age and breadth, it is only about 6-8
> meters tall. It is a butum tree, a kind of pistachio tree to be found
> in our part of the world. (see ACWWP 2008)

The *butum* is a kind of *pistachio* tree of the *anacardiaceous* tree (a family of tropical trees that produce edible drupes). The connection of his analogy to the birth of a common word could be tied to the Greek word *anacardiaceous*. *Ana* means "from" and *kardia* means "heart." It might be said that Prince Ghazi got the inspiration from the heart shape of the fruits of the *butum* tree. In ideography, the shape of heart could be interpreted as *love* in modern sense of meaning-making. Moreover, Prince Ghazi tried to link further the early boyhood of Prophet Muhammad and the Muslims' claims to miracles performed by Prophet Muhammad to have been witnessed by Monk Bahira. He also claimed that Bahira had a book (perhaps the Torah as he thought) that led him to the future Prophet of Islam as extract 8 below portrays:

Extract 8: Eugen Biser Award Ceremony Speech—Prince Ghazi bin Muhammad (3)

> A local Christian monk named Bahira, noticed these two miracles
> from a little distance, and summoned the caravan and the boy, and
> after courteously examining and speaking to him, Bahira witnessed
> the boy as a future Prophet to his people. The monk had a book
> with him that led him to expect a Prophet among the Arabs,
> who were descended from Ishmael the eldest son of the Prophet
> Abraham (peace be upon him). Perhaps it was the Torah, for
> Genesis 49:10 and Deuteronomy 18:15 seem to predict a prophet
> that is not the Messiah and not Judah but from the "brethren" of
> the Jews, but we do not know. (see ACWWP 2008)

Prince Ghazi was sounding anachronistic in his argument and claimed that the prophecy about the coming of Prophet Muhammad was foretold in the Bible (Genesis 49:10 and Deuteronomy 18:15). However, he tried to link the *butum* tree as standing between the Muslim-Christian relations of old and Muslim-Christian relations of new as portrayed in extract 9 below:

Extract 9: Eugen Biser Award Ceremony Speech—Prince Ghazi bin Muhammad (4)

Howbeit, what is most important here is that the selfsame blessed tree underneath which A Common Word was born, also itself gave rise, 1400 years ago to the first harmonious contact between the founder of Islam and Christianity! (see ACWWP 2008)

Chapter Seven

Conclusion

Briefly, the discourses of the conferences, seminars, fora, and workshops yielded fruits that seek to build bridge for cooperation and dialogue between Muslims and Christians. The declarations, final statements, communiqué, and the award speech of Prince Ghazi are indications that what started as a diatribe has eventually become a dialectics between Muslims and Christians. It is on the level of dialectics—as the final declarations, statements, communiqué, and speech portray—that authentic communication between Muslims and Christians should be based. As such, CDA has helped to point out the problem of differences, the ideological issues, and the identity constructions associated with the orthodoxy claims of Tawhid and Trinity.

The analyses from stages 1-4 showed that the people on the grassroots level are in marginality in the entire order of discourses. There is the observation that a common word was structured to be a communication between Muslims and Christians constructed from "above" (religious leaders and scholars of both religions). This makes a common word an interfaith project of intellectuals and spiritual leaders. The construction of identity differs when it comes from "below" (that is, from the grassroots). Therefore, to make a common word more authentic as a means of extending hands of friendship and love of God and neighbor and a way of promoting a multicultural cohesion, the grassroots must be involved. This book suggests educating the young right from kindergarten about this interfaith initiative and going online in various Internet-mediated communications: emails, blogs, chat rooms, focus groups, and fora to create this awareness and put it into practice. This is to put into practice the first plan of action proposed by Cambridge and Lambeth Palace conference communiqué:

> To identify and promote the use of educational materials, for all age-groups and in the widest possible range of languages, that we accept as providing a fair reflection of our faiths. (see ACWWP 2008)

Thus, there is a need to engage Muslims and Christians in social networks like Bebo, YouTube, Facebook, Twitter and the likes. The reason is to start young to disabuse their minds from the bias the Muslims and Christians have for themselves. This reflects point number 13 of the final declaration of the Catholic-Muslim forum:

> Young people are the future of religious communities and of societies as a whole. Increasingly, they will be living in multicultural and multi-religious societies. It is essential that they be well formed in their own religious traditions and well informed about other cultures and religions. (see ACWWP 2008)

Another important way of inculcating the good practice of authentic communication is to go into the sacred scriptures of both the Qur'an and the Bible to examine the areas where both religions have smeared the other.

This might seem very difficult or to some very impossible, but it is here that the ideological formulations of the Tawhid and Trinity are built. The norms of the two religions begin in their scriptures and end in their scriptures. This book suggests that if the proposed "a common word" would help in providing the "public sphere" for authentic communication, this issue of proper rendition and interpretation and understanding of the "other's" sacred scripture is a sine qua non.

From the selected extracts studied, there are noted several constructed dichotomizing identities by both Muslim and Christian religious leaders/ scholars. The White Paper revealed these facts. The very first call in extract 1 to a common word was framed in Tawhid ideology. The *surah Al-'Imran* 3:64 ("come to a common word between us and you") was set to "foreground" the Tawhid orthodoxy as against the Trinity. It quotes the Qur'an and uses the Bible New Testament to substantiate the Tawhidic claims (see appendix A).

> Of God's Unity, God says in the Holy Qur'an: Say: He is God, the One! / God, the Self-Sufficient Besought of all! (*Al-Ikhlas* 112:1-2). Of the necessity of love for God, God says in the Holy Qur'an: So invoke the Name of thy Lord and devote thyself to Him with a complete devotion (*Al-Muzzammil* 73:8). [par. 9]

> In the New Testament, Jesus Christ . . . said: "Hear, O Israel, the Lord our God, the Lord is One. / And you shall love the Lord your God with all your heart, with all your soul, with all your mind, and with all your strength." This is the first commandment . . . (Mk. 12:29-31). [par. 9]

Extract 1 (see appendix A), for example, used words and phrases that featured constructed identities for Muslims by placing emphasis on *value* in Islamic words (*Holy*) and phrases (*Holy Qur'an, common word between us and you*), and the same word *Holy* was not applied to the Christian Bible throughout extract 1. There are instances of *valued* personalities (Prophet Muhammad, *peace be upon him*), and objects (the symbols of the crescent). A common word featured further constructed identities for Muslims by representation. It selected a few Muslim scholars, Ulemas, and religious leaders as authenticating and approving a common word as examined above. This book observed that it was a common word for Muslims first before it became a common word between us Muslims and you Christians.

Significantly, it featured an identity construction of Islam as "peaceful" and seeking "peace"; extract 1 carefully selected obvious intertextuality by directly quoting or reporting what the Bible said about the oneness of God. This was another way to construct monotheistic identity for Muslims. Use of intertextuality randomly labeled extract 1 as constructing identity dichotomies. The fascination in the use of the intertextuality of Deuteronomy 6:4 and the subsequent reported speech of Jesus Christ quoting the same Deuteronomy 6:4 portrayed Jesus Christ as a prophet reacting against Christianity's claim to the Trinity. It constructed a monotheistic identity for Jesus as an admirer of Islamic monotheism. This book noted as well that extract 1 effectively constructed identities by the use of consensual pronouns such as *us* in contradistinction to *you*. This dichotomizes the beliefs of *us Muslims* from the beliefs of *you Christians*.

The Christians themselves followed the ideology of the Trinity in their response to a common word. As it was in extract 1, the Muslims used the two typologies of calendar dating (1428 AH [AH meaning the year of Hegira] and October 13, 2007). But for the Christians, extract 2 (see appendix B) explicitly "backgrounded" the Islamic calendar. In extract 1, 1428 AH was "foregrounded" as counterbalancing the Gregorian calendar (October 13, 2007), which, of course, began with *anno Domini* (in the year of the Lord). However, the text "foregrounds" Jesus Christ in its introduction and emphasizes Jesus Christ as the second person of the Trinity (that is, Jesus

Christ as equal in majesty with God the Father: True God from True God) and messiah (see appendix B).

Moreover, the ideology of the Trinity presented Jesus Christ as the Christian model, teacher, life, way, and truth. The Christians depict themselves as followers of Jesus Christ. From here, the Christians construct their identity to correspond with Christ's injunction: to love God and neighbor. There was identity construction when Christians likened themselves to Jesus Christ by asking for forgiveness of the Crusades and excesses of the war on terror. The Christians tactically referred to Jesus Christ more than the way they referred to God in the text. This could be viewed as *identifying* with Jesus Christ, *identifying* with the second person of the Trinity. It was another way of "foregrounding" the Trinity. The semiotic of the text seems to connect to the ideological networks of practices. The introduction of terminologies like *Crusades* and *war on terror* is viewed by this book as inferring the presence of the symbol of the crescent in extract 1 (between paragraphs 22 and 23; 24 and 28; see appendix A). It noted the different ways groups of Christians and Muslims have come together in the bid to agree mutually on compatible interpretations of their different views in the various conferences and workshops.

The four-point final statement of Yale Workshop and Conference, which was constituted by a consortium of Muslim and Christian religious leaders/ scholars, was resolute about their common agreement upon the unity and absoluteness of God, but it has to be in accordance with the specificity of the individual religion's monotheistic heritage. There was an observation that the word *heritage* insists on the thing handed down by tradition, something that can be said to be inalienably the people's right. It could be said here that the Tawhid and the Trinity are Islamic and Christian heritages respectively.

The Cambridge conference's four-point communiqué sought the promotion of this authentic communication between Muslims and Christians when the conference claimed by its public announcement of their deliberation that "education of all age-groups in the widest possible range of languages" should be a genuine means of understanding one another, especially in matters of faith. The Catholic-Muslim Forum, among other things, in point 10 emphasized the need for both Islam and Christianity to provide education that is very sincere and genuine in teaching the young people about the religious values of the other. Practically, the change of use of pronoun in the fifteen-point final declaration to mean collectivity and a signification of unity of purpose is an apparent commitment to interfaith interrelationship and interdependence. For example, instead of continuing with the *us* and *you*, The Catholic-Muslim Forum preferred *We affirm* (points 4 and 8), *we recognize* (point 9), *we are convinced* (point 10), *we profess* (point 11), *we call* (point 12), *we have agreed* (point 14), *we look forward* (point 15). Drawing from the conclusion given by Blair in his foreword to *A Common Word: Muslims and Christians on Loving God and Neighbor* (2010), there is the observation that: "the work of 'A Common Word' is far from complete. There is still much to be done . . . Yet there is no doubt that 'A Common Word' has the potential to effect radical and positive change in relations between Muslims and Christians" (quoted in Volf et al. 2010).

Appendices

Appendix A

Extract 1: An Open Letter and Call from Muslim Religious Leaders to

[1]

In the Name of God, the Compassionate, the Merciful

[2]

On the Occasion of the *Eid al-Fitr al-Mubarak* 1428 A.H. / October 13th 2007 C.E., and on the One Year Anniversary of the Open Letter of 38 Muslim Scholars to H.H. Pope Benedict XVI,

An Open Letter and Call from Muslim Religious Leaders to:

[3]

His Holiness Pope Benedict XVI,

His All-Holiness Bartholomew I, Patriarch of Constantinople, New Rome,
His Beatitude Theodoros II, Pope and Patriarch of Alexandria and All Africa,
His Beatitude Ignatius IV, Patriarch of Antioch and All the East,
His Beatitude Theophilos III, Patriarch of the Holy City of Jerusalem,
His Beatitude Alexy II, Patriarch of Moscow and All Russia,
His Beatitude Pavle, Patriarch of Belgrade and Serbia,
His Beatitude Daniel, Patriarch of Romania,
His Beatitude Maxim, Patriarch of Bulgaria,
His Beatitude Ilia II, Archbishop of Mtskheta-Tbilisi, Catholicos-Patriarch of All Georgia,
His Beatitude Chrisostomos, Archbishop of Cyprus,
His Beatitude Christodoulos, Archbishop of Athens and All Greece,
His Beatitude Sawa, Metropolitan of Warsaw and All Poland,
His Beatitude Anastasios, Archbishop of Tirana, Duerres and All Albania,
His Beatitude Christoforos, Metropolitan of the Czech and Slovak Republics,

[4]

His Holiness Pope Shenouda III, Pope of Alexandria and Patriarch of All Africa on the Apostolic Throne of St. Mark,
His Beatitude Karekin II, Supreme Patriarch and Catholicos of All Armenians,
His Beatitude Ignatius Zakka I, Patriarch of Antioch and All the East, Supreme Head of the Universal Syrian Orthodox Church,
His Holiness Mar Thoma Didymos I, Catholicos of the East on the Apostolic Throne of St. Thomas and the Malankara Metropolitan,
His Holiness Abune Paulos, Fifth Patriarch and Catholicos of Ethiopia, Echege of the See of St. Tekle Haymanot, Archbishop of Axium,

[5]

His Beatitude Mar Dinkha IV, Patriarch of the Holy Apostolic Catholic Assyrian Church of the East,

[6]

The Most Rev. Rowan Williams, Archbishop of Canterbury,
Rev. Mark S. Hanson, Presiding Bishop of the Evangelical Lutheran Church in America, and President of the Lutheran World Federation,
Rev. George H. Freeman, General Secretary, World Methodist Council,
Rev. David Coffey, President of the Baptist World Alliance,
Rev. Setri Nyomi, General Secretary of the World Alliance of Reformed Churches,

[7]

Rev. Dr. Samuel Kobia, General Secretary, World Council of Churches,
And Leaders of Christian Churches, everywhere....

1

In the Name of God, the Compassionate, the Merciful

A Common Word between Us and You
(Summary and Abridgement)

8

Muslims and Christians together make up well over half of the world's population. Without peace and justice between these two religious communities, there can be no meaningful peace in the world. The future of the world depends on peace between Muslims and Christians.

9

The basis for this peace and understanding already exists. It is part of the very foundational principles of both faiths: love of the One God, and love of the neighbour. These principles are found over and over again in the sacred texts of Islam and Christianity. The Unity of God, the necessity of love for Him, and the necessity of love of the neighbour is thus the common ground between Islam and Christianity. The following are only a few examples:

Of God's Unity, God says in the Holy Qur'an: *Say: He is God, the One! / God, the Self-Sufficient Besought of all! (Al-Ikhlas,* 112:1-2). Of the necessity of love for God, God says in the Holy Qur'an: *So invoke the Name of thy Lord and devote thyself to Him with a complete devotion (Al-Muzzammil,* 73:8). Of the necessity of love for the neighbour, the Prophet Muhammad ﷺ said: *"None of you has faith until you love for your neighbour what you love for yourself."*

In the New Testament, Jesus Christ ﷺ said: *'Hear, O Israel, the Lord our God, the Lord is One. / And you shall love the Lord your God with all your heart, with all your soul, with all your mind, and with all your strength.' This is the first commandment. / And the second, like it, is this: 'You shall love your neighbour as yourself.' There is no other commandment greater than these. "* (Mark 12:29-31)

10

In the Holy Qur'an, God Most High enjoins Muslims to issue the following call to Christians (and Jews—the *People of the Scripture*):

> *Say: O People of the Scripture! Come to a common word between us and you: that we shall worship none but God, and that we shall ascribe no partner unto Him, and that none of us shall take others for lords beside God. And if they turn away, then say: Bear witness that we are they who have surrendered (unto Him). (Aal 'Imran* 3:64)

11

The words: *we shall ascribe no partner unto Him* relate to the Unity of God, and the words: *worship none but God,* relate to being totally devoted to God. Hence they all relate to the *First and Greatest Commandment.* According to one of the oldest and most authoritative commentaries on the Holy Qur'an the words: *that none of us shall take others for lords beside God,* mean 'that none of us should obey the other in disobedience

2

12

to what God has commanded'. This relates to the Second Commandment because justice and freedom of religion are a crucial part of love of the neighbour.

Thus in obedience to the Holy Qur'an, we as Muslims invite Christians to come together with us on the basis of what is common to us, which is also what is most essential to our faith and practice: the *Two Commandments* of love.

ॐ ॐ

3

In the Name of God, the Compassionate, the Merciful,
And may peace and blessings be upon the Prophet Muhammad

A COMMON WORD BETWEEN US AND YOU

In the Name of God, the Compassionate, the Merciful,
Call unto the way of thy Lord with wisdom and fair exhortation, and contend with
them in the fairest way. Lo! thy Lord is Best Aware of him who strayeth from His way,
and He is Best Aware of those who go aright.
(The Holy Qur'an, *Al-Nahl*, 16:125)

(I) LOVE OF GOD

LOVE OF GOD IN ISLAM

The Testimonies of Faith

The central creed of Islam consists of the two testimonies of faith or *Shahadahs*[i], which state that: *There is no god but God, Muhammad is the messenger of God.* These Two Testimonies are the *sine qua non* of Islam. He or she who testifies to them is a Muslim; he or she who denies them is not a Muslim. Moreover, the Prophet Muhammad ﷺ said: *The best remembrance is: 'There is no god but God'* ....[ii]

The Best that All the Prophets have Said

Expanding on *the best remembrance*, the Prophet Muhammad ﷺ also said: *The best that I have said—myself, and the prophets that came before me—is: 'There is no god but God, He Alone, He hath no associate, His is the sovereignty and His is the praise and He hath power over all things'*[iii]. The phrases which follow the First Testimony of faith are all from the Holy Qur'an; each describe a mode of love of God, and devotion to Him.

The words: *He Alone,* remind Muslims that their hearts[iv] must be devoted to God Alone, since God says in the Holy Qur'an: *God hath not assigned unto any man two hearts within his body* (*Al-Ahzab,* 33:4). God is Absolute and therefore devotion to Him must be totally sincere.

The words: *He hath no associate,* remind Muslims that they must love God uniquely, without rivals within their souls, since God says in the Holy Qur'an: *Yet there are men who take rivals unto God: they love them as they should love God. But those of faith are more intense in their love for God* .... (*Al-Baqarah,* 2:165). Indeed, *[T]heir flesh and their hearts soften unto the remembrance of God* .... (*Al-Zumar,* 39:23).

4

19

The words: *His is the sovereignty*, remind Muslims that their minds or their understandings must be totally devoted to God, for *the sovereignty* is precisely everything in creation or existence and everything that the mind can know. And all is in God's Hand, since God says in the Holy Qur'an: *Blessed is He in Whose Hand is the sovereignty, and, He is Able to do all things (Al-Mulk, 67:1).*

20

The words: *His is the praise* remind Muslims that they must be grateful to God and trust Him with all their sentiments and emotions. God says in the Holy Qur'an:

> And if thou wert to ask them: Who created the heavens and the earth, and constrained the sun and the moon (to their appointed work)? they would say: God. How then are they turned away ? / God maketh the provision wide for whom He will of His servants, and straiteneth it for whom (He will). Lo! God is Aware of all things. / And if thou wert to ask them: Who causeth water to come down from the sky, and therewith reviveth the earth after its death ? they verily would say: God. Say: Praise be to God! But most of them have no sense. (Al-'Ankabut, 29:61-63)[v]

For all these bounties and more, human beings must always be truly grateful:

> God is He Who created the heavens and the earth, and causeth water to descend from the sky, thereby producing fruits as food for you, and maketh the ships to be of service unto you, that they may run upon the sea at His command, and hath made of service unto you the rivers; / And maketh the sun and the moon, constant in their courses, to be of service unto you, and hath made of service unto you the night and the day./ And He giveth you of all ye ask of Him, and if ye would count the graces of God ye cannot reckon them. Lo! man is verily a wrong-doer, an ingrate. (Ibrahim, 14:32-34)[vi]

Indeed, the *Fatihah*—which is the *greatest chapter in the Holy Qur'an*[vii]—starts with praise to God:

> In the Name of God, the Infinitely Good, the All-Merciful. /
> Praise be to God, the Lord of the worlds. /
> The Infinitely Good, the All-Merciful. /
> Owner of the Day of Judgement. /
> Thee we worship, and Thee we ask for help. /
> Guide us upon the straight path. /
> The path of those on whom is Thy Grace, not those who deserve anger nor those who are astray. (Al-Fatihah, 1:1-7)

The *Fatihah*, recited at least seventeen times daily by Muslims in the canonical prayers, reminds us of the praise and gratitude due to God for His Attributes of Infinite Goodness and All-Mercifulness, not merely for His Goodness and Mercy to us in this life but ultimately, on the Day of Judgement[viii] when it matters the most and when we hope to be forgiven for our sins. It thus ends with prayers for grace and guidance, so that we might attain—through what begins with praise and gratitude— salvation and *love*, for God says

5

in the Holy Qur'an: *Lo! those who believe and do good works, the Infinitely Good will appoint for them love.* (*Maryam*, 19:96)

21

The words: *and He hath power over all things,* remind Muslims that they must be mindful of God's Omnipotence and thus fear God[ix]. God says in the Holy Qur'an:

> ... *[A]nd fear God, and know that God is with the God-fearing. / Spend your wealth for the cause of God, and be not cast by your own hands to ruin; and do good. Lo! God loveth the virtuous. / .... (Al-Baqarah,* 2:194-5)...
> *[A]nd fear God, and know that God is severe in punishment. (Al-Baqarah,* 2:196)

22

Through fear of God, the actions, might and strength of Muslims should be totally devoted to God. God says in the Holy Qur'an:

> ...*[A]nd know that God is with those who fear Him. (Al-Tawbah,* 9:36) ....
> *O ye who believe! What aileth you that when it is said unto you: Go forth in the way of God, ye are bowed down to the ground with heaviness. Take ye pleasure in the life of the world rather than in the Hereafter? The comfort of the life of the world is but little in the Hereafter. / If ye go not forth He will afflict you with a painful doom, and will choose instead of you a folk other than you. Ye cannot harm Him at all. God is Able to do all things. (Al-Tawbah,* 9:38-39)

☾

23

The words: *His is the sovereignty and His is the praise and He hath power over all things,* when taken all together, remind Muslims that just as everything in creation glorifies God, everything that is in their souls must be devoted to God:

> *All that is in the heavens and all that is in the earth glorifieth God; His is the sovereignty and His is the praise and He hath power over all things.* (*Al-Taghabun,* 64:1)

For indeed, all that is in people's souls is known, and accountable, to God:

> *He knoweth all that is in the heavens and the earth, and He knoweth what ye conceal and what ye publish. And God is Aware of what is in the breasts (of men). (Al-Taghabun,* 64:4)

24

As we can see from all the passages quoted above, souls are depicted in the Holy Qur'an as having three main faculties: the mind or the intelligence, which is made for comprehending the truth; the will which is made for freedom of choice, and sentiment which is made for loving the good and the beautiful[x]. Put in another way, we could say that man's soul knows through *understanding* the truth, through *willing* the good, and through virtuous emotions and *feeling* love for God. Continuing in the same chapter of the Holy Qur'an (as that quoted above), God orders people to fear Him as much as possible, and to listen (and thus to understand the truth); to obey (and thus to will the good), and to spend (and thus to exercise love and virtue), which, He says, is better for

6

our souls. By engaging *everything* in our souls—the faculties of knowledge, will, and love—we may come to be purified and attain ultimate success:

> *So fear God as best ye can, and listen, and obey, and spend; that is better*
> *for your souls. And those who are saved from the pettiness of their own*
> *souls, such are the successful. (Al-Taghabun, 64:16)*

☾

| 25 |

In summary then, when the entire phrase *He Alone, He hath no associate, His is the sovereignty and His is the praise and He hath power over all things* is added to the testimony of faith—*There is no god but God*—it reminds Muslims that their hearts, their individual souls and all the faculties and powers of their souls (or simply their *entire* hearts and souls) must be totally devoted and attached to God. Thus God says to the Prophet Muhammad ﷺ in the Holy Qur'an:

> *Say: Lo! my worship and my sacrifice and my living and my dying are for*
> *God, Lord of the Worlds. / He hath no partner. This am I commanded, and*
> *I am first of those who surrender (unto Him). / Say: Shall I seek another*
> *than God for Lord, when He is Lord of all things? Each soul earneth only*
> *on its own account, nor doth any laden bear another's load.... (Al-An'am,*
> *6:162-164)*

| 26 |

These verses epitomize the Prophet Muhammad's ﷺ complete and utter devotion to God. Thus in the Holy Qur'an God enjoins Muslims who truly love God to follow this example[xi], in order in turn to be loved[xii] by God:

> *Say, (O Muhammad, to mankind): If ye love God, follow me; God will love*
> *you and forgive you your sins. God is Forgiving, Merciful. (Aal 'Imran,*
> *3:31)*

| 27 |

Love of God in Islam is thus part of complete and total devotion to God; it is not a mere fleeting, partial emotion. As seen above, God commands in the Holy Qur'an: *Say: Lo! my worship and my sacrifice and my living and my dying are for God, Lord of the Worlds. / He hath no partner.* The call to be totally devoted and attached to God heart and soul, far from being a call for a mere emotion or for a mood, is in fact an injunction requiring all-embracing, constant and active love of God. It demands a love in which the innermost spiritual heart and the whole of the soul—with its intelligence, will and feeling—participate through devotion.

☾

None Comes with Anything Better

| 28 |

We have seen how the blessed phrase: *There is no god but God, He Alone, He hath no associate, His is the sovereignty and His is the praise and He hath power over all things*—which is the best that all the prophets have said—makes explicit what is implicit

7

in *the best remembrance (There is no god but God)* by showing what it requires and entails, by way of devotion. It remains to be said that this blessed formula is also in itself a sacred invocation—a kind of extension of the First Testimony of faith *(There is no god but God)*—the ritual repetition of which can bring about, through God's grace, some of the devotional attitudes it demands, namely, loving and being devoted to God with all one's heart, all one's soul, all one's mind, all one's will or strength, and all one's sentiment. Hence the Prophet Muhammad ﷺ commended this remembrance by saying:

> He who says: 'There is no god but God, He Alone, He hath no associate, His is the sovereignty and His is the praise and He hath power over all things' one hundred times in a day, it is for them equal to setting ten slaves free, and one hundred good deeds are written for them and one hundred bad deeds are effaced, and it is for them a protection from the devil for that day until the evening. And none offers anything better than that, save one who does more than that.[xiii]

29

In other words, the blessed remembrance, *There is no god but God, He Alone, He hath no associate, His is the sovereignty and His is the praise and He hath power over all things,* not only requires and implies that Muslims must be totally devoted to God and love Him with their whole hearts and their whole souls and all that is in them, but provides a way, like its beginning (the testimony of faith)—through its frequent repetition[xiv]—for them to realize this love with everything they are.

30

God says in one of the very first revelations in the Holy Qur'an: *So invoke the Name of thy Lord and devote thyself to Him with a complete devotion (Al-Muzzammil,* 73:8). ✪

LOVE OF GOD AS THE *FIRST AND GREATEST COMMANDMENT* IN THE BIBLE

31

The *Shema* in the Book of Deuteronomy (6:4-5), a centrepiece of the Old Testament and of Jewish liturgy, says: *Hear, O Israel: The LORD our God, the LORD is one! / You shall love the LORD your God with all your heart, and with all your soul, and with all your strength.*[xv]

32

Likewise, in the New Testament, when Jesus Christ, the Messiah ﷺ, is asked about the Greatest Commandment, he answers ﷺ:

> But when the Pharisees heard that he had silenced the Sadducees, they gathered together. / Then one of them, a lawyer, asked Him a question, testing Him, and saying, / "Teacher, which is the great commandment in the law?" / Jesus said to him, " 'You shall love the LORD your God with all your heart, with all your soul, and with all your mind.' / This is the first and greatest commandment. / And the second is like it: 'You shall love your neighbour as yourself.' / On these two commandments hang all the Law and the Prophets." (Matthew 22:34-40)

8

And also:

Then one of the scribes came, and having heard them reasoning together, perceiving that he had answered them well, asked him, "Which is the first commandment of all?" / Jesus answered him, "The first of all the commandments is: 'Hear, O Israel, the LORD our God, the LORD is one. / And you shall love the LORD your God with all your heart, with all your soul, with all your mind, and with all your strength.' This is the first commandment. / And the second, like it, is this: 'You shall love your neighbour as yourself.' There is no other commandment greater than these." (Mark 12:28-31)

33

The commandment to love God fully is thus the *First and Greatest Commandment* of the Bible. Indeed, it is to be found in a number of other places throughout the Bible including: Deuteronomy 4:29, 10:12, 11:13 (also part of the *Shema*), 13:3, 26:16, 30:2, 30:6, 30:10; Joshua 22:5; Mark 12:32-33 and Luke 10:27-28.

34

However, in various places throughout the Bible, it occurs in slightly different forms and versions. For instance, in Matthew 22:37 (*You shall love the LORD your God with all your heart, with all your soul, and with all your mind*), the Greek word for "heart" is *kardia*, the word for "soul" is *psyche*, and the word for "mind" is *dianoia*. In the version from Mark 12:30 (*And you shall love the LORD your God with all your heart, with all your soul, with all your mind, and with all your strength*) the word "strength" is added to the aforementioned three, translating the Greek word *ischus*.

35

The words of the lawyer in Luke 10:27 (which are confirmed by Jesus Christ ﷺ in Luke 10:28) contain the same four terms as Mark 12:30. The words of the scribe in Mark 12:32 (which are approved of by Jesus Christ ﷺ in Mark 12:34) contain the three terms *kardia* ("heart"), *dianoia* ("mind"), and *ischus* ("strength").

36

In the *Shema* of Deuteronomy 6:4-5 (*Hear, O Israel: The LORD our God, the LORD is one! / You shall love the LORD your God with all your heart, and with all your soul, and with all your strength*). In Hebrew the word for "heart" is *lev*, the word for "soul" is *nefesh*, and the word for "strength" is *me'od*.

37

In Joshua 22:5, the Israelites are commanded by Joshua ﷺ to love God and be devoted to Him as follows:

"But take careful heed to do the commandment and the law which Moses the servant of the LORD commanded you, to love the LORD your God, to walk in all His ways, to keep His commandments, to hold fast to Him, and to serve Him with all your heart and with all your soul." (Joshua 22:5)

38

What all these versions thus have in common—despite the language differences between the Hebrew Old Testament, the original words of Jesus Christ ﷺ in Aramaic, and the actual transmitted Greek of the New Testament—is the command to love God fully with one's heart and soul and to be fully devoted to Him. This is the First and Greatest Commandment for human beings. ✳

9

39

      In the light of what we have seen to be necessarily implied and evoked by the Prophet Muhammad's ﷺ blessed saying: *'The best that I have said—myself, and the prophets that came before me*—is: *'There is no god but God, He Alone, He hath no associate, His is the sovereignty and His is the praise and He hath power over all things'* [xvi], we can now perhaps understand the words *'The best that I have said—myself, and the prophets that came before me'* as equating the blessed formula *'There is no god but God, He Alone, He hath no associate, His is the sovereignty and His is the praise and He hath power over all things'* precisely with the 'First and Greatest Commandment' to love God, with all one's heart and soul, as found in various places in the Bible. That is to say, in other words, that the Prophet Muhammad ﷺ was perhaps, through inspiration, restating and alluding to the Bible's First Commandment. God knows best, but certainly we have seen their effective similarity in meaning. Moreover, we also do know (as can be seen in the endnotes), that both formulas have another remarkable parallel: the way they arise in a number of slightly differing versions and forms in different contexts, all of which, nevertheless, emphasize the primacy of total love and devotion to God [xvii].

☙ ❧

10

(II) LOVE OF THE NEIGHBOUR

LOVE OF THE NEIGHBOUR IN ISLAM

[40] There are numerous injunctions in Islam about the necessity and paramount importance of love for—and mercy towards—the neighbour. Love of the neighbour is an essential and integral part of faith in God and love of God because in Islam without love of the neighbour there is no true faith in God and no righteousness. The Prophet Muhammad ﷺ said: *"None of you has faith until you love for your brother what you love for yourself."*[xviii] And: *"None of you has faith until you love for your neighbour what you love for yourself."*[xxix]

[41] However, empathy and sympathy for the neighbour—and even formal prayers— are not enough. They must be accompanied by generosity and self-sacrifice. God says in the Holy Qur'an:

> *It is not righteousness that ye turn your faces*[xx] *to the East and the West; but righteous is he who believeth in God and the Last Day and the angels and the Scripture and the prophets; and giveth wealth, for love of Him, to kinsfolk and to orphans and the needy and the wayfarer and to those who ask, and to set slaves free; and observeth proper worship and payeth the poor-due. And those who keep their treaty when they make one, and the patient in tribulation and adversity and time of stress. Such are they who are sincere. Such are the pious. (Al-Baqarah 2:177)*

And also:

> *Ye will not attain unto righteousness until ye expend of that which ye love. And whatsoever ye expend, God is Aware thereof. (Aal 'Imran, 3:92)*

[42] Without giving the neighbour what we ourselves love, we do not truly love God or the neighbour. ✿

LOVE OF THE NEIGHBOUR IN THE BIBLE

[43] We have already cited the words of the Messiah, Jesus Christ ﷺ, about the paramount importance, second only to the love of God, of the love of the neighbour:

> *This is the first and greatest commandment. / And the second is like it: 'You shall love your neighbour as yourself.' / On these two commandments hang all the Law and the Prophets. (Matthew 22:38-40)*

And:

11

*And the second, like it, is this: 'You shall love your neighbour as yourself.'
There is no other commandment greater than these."* (Mark 12:31)

44

It remains only to be noted that this commandment is also to be found in the Old Testament:

*You shall not hate your brother in your heart. You shall surely rebuke
your neighbour, and not bear sin because of him. / You shall not take
vengeance, nor bear any grudge against the children of your people, but
you shall love your neighbour as yourself: I am the LORD.* (Leviticus
19:17-18)

45

Thus the Second Commandment, like the First Commandment, demands generosity and self-sacrifice, and *On these two commandments hang all the Law and the Prophets.* ✳

12

(III) *COME TO A COMMON WORD BETWEEN US AND YOU*

A Common Word

46

Whilst Islam and Christianity are obviously different religions—and whilst there is no minimising some of their formal differences—it is clear that the *Two Greatest Commandments* are an area of common ground and a link between the Qur'an, the Torah and the New Testament. What prefaces the Two Commandments in the Torah and the New Testament, and what they arise out of, is the Unity of God—that there is only one God. For the *Shema* in the Torah, starts: (Deuteronomy 6:4) *Hear, O Israel: The LORD our God, the LORD is one!* Likewise, Jesus 🕮 said: (Mark 12:29) *"The first of all the commandments is: 'Hear, O Israel, the LORD our God, the LORD is one"*. Likewise, God says in the Holy Qur'an: *Say: He, God, is One. / God, the Self-Sufficient Besought of all. (Al-Ikhlas,* 112:1-2). Thus the Unity of God, love of Him, and love of the neighbour form a common ground upon which Islam and Christianity (and Judaism) are founded.

47

This could not be otherwise since Jesus 🕮 said: (Matthew 22:40)*"On these two commandments hang all the Law and the Prophets."* Moreover, God confirms in the Holy Qur'an that the Prophet Muhammad 🕮 brought nothing fundamentally or essentially new: *Naught is said to thee (Muhammad) but what already was said to the messengers before thee (Fussilat* 41:43). And: *Say (Muhammad): I am no new thing among the messengers (of God), nor know I what will be done with me or with you. I do but follow that which is Revealed to me, and I am but a plain warner (Al-Ahqaf,* 46:9). Thus also God in the Holy Qur'an confirms that the same eternal truths of the Unity of God, of the necessity for total love and devotion to God (and thus shunning false gods), and of the necessity for love of fellow human beings (and thus justice), underlie all true religion:

> *And verily We have raised in every nation a messenger, (proclaiming): Worship God and shun false gods. Then some of them (there were) whom God guided, and some of them (there were) upon whom error had just hold. Do but travel in the land and see the nature of the consequence for the deniers! (Al-Nahl,* 16:36)
> *We verily sent Our messengers with clear proofs, and revealed with them the Scripture and the Balance, that mankind may stand forth in justice....* (Al-Hadid, 57:25)

Come to a Common Word!

48

In the Holy Qur'an, God Most High tells Muslims to issue the following call to Christians (and Jews—the *People of the Scripture*):

> *Say: O People of the Scripture! Come to a common word between us and you: that we shall worship none but God, and that we shall ascribe no partner unto Him, and that none of us shall take others for lords beside*

13

49

God. And if they turn away, then say: Bear witness that we are they who have surrendered (unto Him). (Aal 'Imran 3:64)

Clearly, the blessed words: *we shall ascribe no partner unto Him* relate to the Unity of God. Clearly also, worshipping *none but God*, relates to being totally devoted to God and hence to the *First and Greatest Commandment.* According to one of the oldest and most authoritative commentaries (*tafsir*) on the Holy Qur'an—the *Jami' Al-Bayan fi Ta'wil Al-Qur'an* of Abu Ja'far Muhammad bin Jarir Al-Tabari (d. 310 A.H. / 923 C.E.)—*that none of us shall take others for lords beside God*, means 'that none of us should obey in disobedience to what God has commanded, nor glorify them by prostrating to them in the same way as they prostrate to God'. In other words, that Muslims, Christians and Jews should be free to each follow what God commanded them, and not have 'to prostrate before kings and the like'[xxi]; for God says elsewhere in the Holy Qur'an: *Let there be no compulsion in religion....* (*Al-Baqarah*, 2:256). This clearly relates to the Second Commandment and to love of the neighbour of which justice[xxii] and freedom of religion are a crucial part. God says in the Holy Qur'an:

God forbiddeth you not those who warred not against you on account of religion and drove you not out from your homes, that ye should show them kindness and deal justly with them. Lo! God loveth the just dealers. (Al-Mumtahinah, 60:8)

☙ ❧

50

We thus as Muslims invite Christians to remember Jesus's ﷺ words in the Gospel (Mark 12:29-31):

... the LORD our God, the LORD is one. / And you shall love the LORD your God with all your heart, with all your soul, with all your mind, and with all your strength.' This is the first commandment. / And the second, like it, is this: 'You shall love your neighbour as yourself.' There is no other commandment greater than these.

51

As Muslims, we say to Christians that we are not against them and that Islam is not against them—so long as they do not wage war against Muslims on account of their religion, oppress them and drive them out of their homes, (in accordance with the verse of the Holy Qur'an [*Al-Mumtahinah*, 60:8] quoted above). Moreover, God says in the Holy Qur'an:

They are not all alike. Of the People of the Scripture there is a staunch community who recite the revelations of God in the night season, falling prostrate (before Him). / They believe in God and the Last Day, and enjoin right conduct and forbid indecency, and vie one with another in good works. These are of the righteous. / And whatever good they do, nothing will be rejected of them. God is Aware of those who ward off (evil). (Aal-'Imran, 3:113-115)

14

Is Christianity necessarily against Muslims? In the Gospel Jesus Christ 鐵 says:

He who is not with me is against me, and he who does not gather with me
scatters abroad. (Matthew 12:30)
For he who is not against us is on our side. (Mark 9:40)
... for he who is not against us is on our side. (Luke 9:50)

According to the *Blessed Theophylact's*[xxiii] *Explanation of the New Testament*, these statements are not contradictions because the first statement (in the actual Greek text of the New Testament) refers to demons, whereas the second and third statements refer to people who recognised Jesus, but were not Christians. Muslims recognize Jesus Christ as the Messiah, not in the same way Christians do (but Christians themselves anyway have never all agreed with each other on Jesus Christ's 鐵 nature), but in the following way: *.... the Messiah Jesus son of Mary is a Messenger of God and His Word which he cast unto Mary and a Spirit from Him....* (*Al-Nisa'*, 4:171). We therefore invite Christians to consider Muslims *not against* and thus *with them*, in accordance with Jesus Christ's 鐵 words here.

[52]

Finally, as Muslims, and in obedience to the Holy Qur'an, we ask Christians to come together with us on the common essentials of our two religions ... *that we shall worship none but God, and that we shall ascribe no partner unto Him, and that none of us shall take others for lords beside God* ... (*Aal 'Imran*, 3:64).

[53]

Let this common ground be the basis of all future interfaith dialogue between us, for our common ground is that on which hangs *all the Law and the Prophets* (Matthew 22:40). God says in the Holy Qur'an:

Say (O Muslims): We believe in God and that which is revealed unto us
and that which was revealed unto Abraham, and Ishmael, and Isaac, and
Jacob, and the tribes, and that which Moses and Jesus received, and that
which the prophets received from their Lord. We make no distinction
between any of them, and unto Him we have surrendered. / And if they
believe in the like of that which ye believe, then are they rightly guided.
But if they turn away, then are they in schism, and God will suffice thee
against them. He is the Hearer, the Knower. (*Al-Baqarah*, 2:136-137)

Between Us and You

[54]

Finding common ground between Muslims and Christians is not simply a matter for polite ecumenical dialogue between selected religious leaders. Christianity and Islam are the largest and second largest religions in the world and in history. Christians and Muslims reportedly make up over a third and over a fifth of humanity respectively. Together they make up more than 55% of the world's population, making the relationship between these two religious communities the most important factor in contributing to meaningful peace around the world. If Muslims and Christians are not at peace, the world cannot be at peace. With the terrible weaponry of the modern world; with Muslims and

15

Christians intertwined everywhere as never before, no side can unilaterally win a conflict between more than half of the world's inhabitants. Thus our common future is at stake. The very survival of the world itself is perhaps at stake.

55

And to those who nevertheless relish conflict and destruction for their own sake or reckon that ultimately they stand to gain through them, we say that our very eternal souls are all also at stake if we fail to sincerely make every effort to make peace and come together in harmony. God says in the Holy Qur'an: *Lo! God enjoineth justice and kindness, and giving to kinsfolk, and forbiddeth lewdness and abomination and wickedness. He exhorteth you in order that ye may take heed (Al Nahl,* 16:90). Jesus Christ ﷺ said: *Blessed are the peacemakers ....*(Matthew 5:9), and also: *For what profit is it to a man if he gains the whole world and loses his soul?* (Matthew 16:26).

56

So let our differences not cause hatred and strife between us. Let us vie with each other only in righteousness and good works. Let us respect each other, be fair, just and kind to another and live in sincere peace, harmony and mutual goodwill. God says in the Holy Qur'an:

> And unto thee have We revealed the Scripture with the truth, confirming whatever Scripture was before it, and a watcher over it. So judge between them by that which God hath revealed, and follow not their desires away from the truth which hath come unto thee. For each We have appointed a law and a way. Had God willed He could have made you one community. But that He may try you by that which He hath given you (He hath made you as ye are). So vie one with another in good works. Unto God ye will all return, and He will then inform you of that wherein ye differ. (Al-Ma'idah, 5:48)

Wal-Salaamu 'Alaykum,
Pax Vobiscum.

© 2007 C.E., 1428 A.H.,
The Royal Aal al-Bayt Institute for Islamic Thought, Jordan.
See: www.acommonword.org or: www.acommonword.com

16

Appendix B
Extract 2: Loving God and Neighbor Together: A Christian Response to *A Common Word Between Us and You*

"THE YALE RESPONSE"

"THE YALE RESPONSE"

*Response of over 300 leading Christian Scholars
to A Common Word published as a full page
advertisement in the* New York Times

13th October 2007 & 18th November 2007

───

*In the name of the Infinitely Good God
whom we should love with all our being*

Loving God and Neighbor Together:
A Christian Response to
A Common Word Between Us and You

[1]

[On October 13, 2007, on the occasion of Eid al-Fitr, 138 Muslim scholars and clerics sent an open letter "to leaders of Christian churches, everywhere." The signatories to that letter, titled A Common Word Between Us and You, *include top leaders from around the world representing every major school of Islamic thought ...*

[2]

The following response was drafted by scholars at Yale Divinity School's Center for Faith and Culture. It was issued by the first four signatories* below and endorsed by almost 300 other Christian theologians and leaders, including those listed here. To promote constructive engagement between these major religious communities, planning is under-

82

"THE YALE RESPONSE"

way for a series of major conferences and workshops involving many of the signatories to A Common Word *and to the Yale response, as well as other international Christian, Muslim, and Jewish leaders ...]*

Preamble

3

As members of the worldwide Christian community, we were deeply encouraged and challenged by the recent historic open letter signed by 138 leading Muslim scholars, clerics, and intellectuals from around the world. *A Common Word Between Us and You* identifies some core common ground between Christianity and Islam which lies at the heart of our respective faiths as well as at the heart of the most ancient Abrahamic faith, Judaism. Jesus Christ's call to love God and neighbor was rooted in the divine revelation to the people of Israel embodied in the Torah (Deuteronomy 6:5; Leviticus 19:18). We receive the open letter as a Muslim hand of conviviality and cooperation extended to Christians worldwide. In this response we extend our own Christian hand in return, so that together with all other human beings we may live in peace and justice as we seek to love God and our neighbors.

4

Muslims and Christians have not always shaken

83

A COMMON WORD

hands in friendship; their relations have sometimes been tense, even characterized by outright hostility. Since Jesus Christ says, "First take the log out your own eye, and then you will see clearly to take the speck out of your neighbor's eye" (Matthew 7:5), we want to begin by acknowledging that in the past (e.g. in the Crusades) and in the present (e.g. in excesses of the "war on terror") many Christians have been guilty of sinning against our Muslim neighbors. Before we "shake your hand" in responding to your letter, we ask forgiveness of the All-Merciful One and of the Muslim community around the world.

Religious Peace—World Peace
5
"Muslims and Christians together make up well over half of the world's population. Without peace and justice between these two religious communities, there can be no meaningful peace in the world." We share the sentiment of the Muslim signatories expressed in these opening lines of their open letter. Peaceful relations between Muslims and Christians stand as one of the central challenges of this century, and perhaps of the whole present epoch. Though tensions, conflicts, and even wars in which Christians and Muslims stand against each other are not primarily religious in character, they possess an

84

"THE YALE RESPONSE"

undeniable religious dimension. If we can achieve religious peace between these two religious communities, peace in the world will clearly be easier to attain. It is therefore no exaggeration to say, as you have in *A Common Word Between Us and You*, that "the future of the world depends on peace between Muslims and Christians."

Common Ground

6

What is so extraordinary about *A Common Word Between Us and You* is not that its signatories recognize the critical character of the present moment in relations between Muslims and Christians. It is rather a deep insight and courage with which they have identified the common ground between the Muslim and Christian religious communities. What is common between us lies not in something marginal nor in something merely important to each. It lies, rather, in something absolutely central to both: love of God and love of neighbor. Surprisingly for many Christians, your letter considers the dual command of love to be the foundational principle not just of the Christian faith, but of Islam as well. That *so much* common ground exists—common ground in some of the fundamentals of faith—gives hope that undeniable differences and even the very real external pressures that

85

A COMMON WORD

bear down upon us can not overshadow the common ground upon which we stand together. That this common ground consists in *love* of God and of neighbor gives hope that deep cooperation between us can be a hallmark of the relations between our two communities.

Love of God

7

We applaud that *A Common Word Between Us and You* stresses so insistently the unique devotion to one God, indeed the love of God, as the primary duty of every believer. God alone rightly commands our ultimate allegiance. When anyone or anything besides God commands our ultimate allegiance—a ruler, a nation, economic progress, or anything else—we end up serving idols and inevitably get mired in deep and deadly conflicts.

8

We find it equally heartening that the God whom we should love above all things is described as being Love. In the Muslim tradition, God, "the Lord of the worlds," is "The Infinitely Good and All-Merciful." And the New Testament states clearly that "God is love" (1 John 4:8). Since God's goodness is infinite and not bound by anything, God "makes his sun rise on the evil and the good, and sends rain on the righteous and the unrighteous," according to the words of Jesus Christ recorded in the Gospel (Matthew 5:45).

86

"THE YALE RESPONSE"

9

For Christians, humanity's love of God and God's love of humanity are intimately linked. As we read in the New Testament: "We love because he [God] first loved us" (1 John 4:19). Our love of God springs from and is nourished by God's love for us. It cannot be otherwise, since the Creator who has power over all things is infinitely good.

Love of Neighbor

10

We find deep affinities with our own Christian faith when *A Common Word Between Us and You* insists that love is the pinnacle of our duties toward our neighbors. "None of you has faith until you love for your neighbor what you love for yourself," the Prophet Muhammad said. In the New Testament we similarly read, "whoever does not love [the neighbor] does not know God" (1 John 4:8) and "whoever does not love his brother whom he has seen cannot love God whom he has not seen" (1 John 4:20). God is love, and our highest calling as human beings is to imitate the One whom we worship.

11

We applaud when you state that "justice and freedom of religion are a crucial part" of the love of neighbor. When justice is lacking, neither love of God nor love of the neighbor can be present. When freedom to worship God according to one's conscience is curtailed, God is

87

A COMMON WORD

dishonored, the neighbor oppressed, and neither God nor neighbor is loved.

12 Since Muslims seek to love their Christian neighbors, they are not against them, the document encouragingly states. Instead, Muslims are *with* them. As Christians we resonate deeply with this sentiment. Our faith teaches that we must be with our neighbors—indeed, that we must act in their favor—even when our neighbors turn out to be our enemies. "But I say unto you," says Jesus Christ, "Love your enemies and pray for those who persecute you, so that you may be children of your Father in heaven; for he makes his sun rise on the evil and on the good" (Matthew 5:44-45). Our love, Jesus Christ says, must imitate the love of the infinitely good Creator; our love must be as unconditional as is God's—extending to brothers, sisters, neighbors, and even enemies. At the end of his life, Jesus Christ himself prayed for his enemies: "Forgive them; for they do not know what they are doing" (Luke 23:34).

13 The Prophet Muhammad did similarly when he was violently rejected and stoned by the people of Ta'if. He is known to have said, "The most virtuous behavior is to engage those who sever relations, to give to those who withhold from you, and to forgive those who wrong you." (It is perhaps significant that after the Prophet

88

"THE YALE RESPONSE"

Muhammad was driven out of Ta'if, it was the Christian slave 'Addas who went out to Muhammad, brought him food, kissed him, and embraced him.)

The Task Before Us

14

"Let this common ground"—the dual common ground of love of God and of neighbor—"be the basis of all future interfaith dialogue between us," your courageous letter urges. Indeed, in the generosity with which the letter is written you embody what you call for. We most heartily agree. Abandoning all "hatred and strife," we must engage in interfaith dialogue as those who seek each other's good, for the one God unceasingly seeks our good. Indeed, together with you we believe that we need to move beyond "a polite ecumenical dialogue between selected religious leaders" and work diligently together to reshape relations between our communities and our nations so that they genuinely reflect our common love for God and for one another.

15

Given the deep fissures in the relations between Christians and Muslims today, the task before us is daunting. And the stakes are great. The future of the world depends on our ability as Christians and Muslims to live together in peace. If we fail to make every effort to make peace and come together in harmony you correctly

89

---

remind us that "our eternal souls" are at stake as well.

We are persuaded that our next step should be for our leaders at every level to meet together and begin the earnest work of determining how God would have us fulfill the requirement that we love God and one another. It is with humility and hope that we receive your generous letter, and we commit ourselves to labor together in heart, soul, mind and strength for the objectives you so appropriately propose.

* Harold W. Attridge, *Dean and Lillian Claus Professor of New Testament, Yale Divinity School*
* Miroslav Volf, *Founder and Director of the Yale Center for Faith and Culture, Henry B. Wright Professor of Theology, Yale University*
* Joseph Cumming, *Director of the Reconciliation Program, Yale Center for Faith and Culture*
* Emilie M. Townes, *Andrew Mellon Professor of African American Religion and Theology and president-elect of the American Academy of Religion*

List of endorsements as published in the New York Times *advert on 18 November 2007:*

Martin Accad, *Academic Dean, Arab Baptist Theological Seminary (Lebanon)*
Scott C. Alexander, *Director, Catholic-Muslim Studies, Catholic Theological Union*
Roger Allen, *Chair, Department of Near Eastern Languages and Civilizations, University of Pennsylvania*

90

1. For Christians the source and example of love of God and neighbor is the love of Christ for his Father, for humanity and for each person. God is Love (I Jn 4:16) and "God so loved the world that He gave his only Son so that whoever believes in him shall not perish but have eternal life" (Jn 3:16). God's love is placed in the human heart through the Holy Spirit. It is God who first loves us thereby enabling us to love Him in return. Love does not harm one's neighbor but rather seeks to do to the other what one would want done to oneself (Cf. I Cor. 13:4-7). Love is the foundation and sum of all the commandments (Cf. Gal 5:14). Love of neighbor cannot be separated from love of God, because it is an expression of our love for God. This is the new commandment; Love one another as I have loved you. (Jn 15:12) Grounded in Christ's sacrificial love, Christian love is forgiving and excludes no one; it therefore also includes one's enemies. It should be not just words but deeds (Cf. I Jn 4:18). This is the sign of its genuineness. For Muslims, as set out in A Common Word, love is a timeless transcendent power which guides and transforms human mutual regard. This love, as indicated by the Holy and Beloved Prophet Muhammad, is prior to the human love for the One True God. A Hadith indicates that God's loving compassion for humanity is even greater than that of a mother for her child (Muslim, Bab al Tawba: 21); it therefore exists before and independently of the human response to the One who is 'The Loving'. So immense is this love and compassion that God has intervened to guide and save humanity in a perfect way many times and in many places, by sending prophets and scriptures. The last of these books, the Qur'an, portrays a world of signs, a marvelous cosmos of Divine artistry, which calls forth our utter love and devotion, so that 'those

who have faith, have most love of God' (2:165), and 'those that believe, and do good works, the Merciful shall engender love among them.' (19:96) In a Hadith we read that 'Not one of you has faith until he loves for his neighbor what he loves for himself' (Bukhari, Bab al Iman: 13).

2. Human life is a most precious gift of God to each person. It should therefore be preserved and honored in all its stages.

3. Human dignity is derived from the fact that every human person is created by a loving God, and has been endowed with the gifts of reason and freewill, and therefore enabled to love God and others. On the firm basis of these principles, the person requires the respect of his or her original dignity and his or her human vocation. Therefore, he or she is entitled to full recognition of his or her identity and freedom by individuals, communities and governments, supported by civil legislation that assures equal rights and full citizenship.

4. We affirm that God's creation of humanity has two great aspects: the male and the female human person and we commit ourselves jointly to ensuring that human dignity and respect are extended on an equal basis to both men and women.

5. Genuine love of neighbor implies respect of the person and her or his choices in matters of conscience and religion. It includes the right of individuals and communities to practice their religion in private and public.

6. Religious minorities are entitled to be respected in their own religious convictions and practices. They are also entitled to their own places of worship, and their founding figures and symbols they consider sacred should not be subject to any form of mockery or ridicule.

7. As Catholic and Muslim believers, we are aware of the summons and imperative to bear witness to the transcendent dimension of life, through a spirituality nourished by prayer, in a world which is becoming more and more secularized and materialistic.

8. We affirm that no religion and its followers should be excluded from society. Each should be able to make its indispensable contribution to the good of society, especially in service to the most needy.

9. We recognize that God's creation in its plurality of cultures, civilizations, languages and peoples is a source of richness and should therefore never become a cause of tension and conflict.

10. We are convinced that Catholics and Muslims have the duty to provide a sound education in human, civic, religious and moral values for their respective members and to promote accurate information about each other's religions.

11. We profess that Catholics and Muslims are called to be instruments of love and harmony among believers, and for humanity as a whole, renouncing any oppression, aggressive violence and terrorism, especially that were committed in the name of religion, and upholding the principle of justice for all.

12. We call upon believers to work for an ethical financial system in which the regulatory mechanisms consider the situation of the poor and disadvantaged, both as individuals, and as indebted nations. We call upon the privileged of the world to consider the plight of those afflicted most severely by the current crisis in food production and distribution, and ask religious believers of all denominations and all people of good will to

work together to alleviate the suffering of the hungry, and to eliminate its causes.

13. Young people are the future of religious communities and of societies as a whole. Increasingly, they will be living in multicultural and multi-religious societies. It is essential that they be well formed in their own religious traditions and well informed about other cultures and religions.

14. We have agreed to explore the possibility of establishing a permanent Catholic Muslim committee to coordinate responses to conflicts and other emergency situations.

15. We look forward to the second Seminar of the Catholic Muslim Forum to be convened in approximately two years in a Muslim majority country yet to be determined. All participants felt gratitude to God for the gift of their time together and for an enriching exchange. At the end of the Seminar His Holiness Pope Benedict XVI received the participants and, following addresses by Professor Dr. Seyyed Hossein Nasr and H.E. Grand Mufti Dr. Mustafa Ceric, spoke to the group. All present expressed satisfaction with the results of the Seminar and their expectation for further productive dialogue.

Notes

1   A Common Word was originated by Ghazi bin Muhammad. (See *The Official Website of A Common Word*, 13 October 2007, *http://www.acommonword.com* Any reference to this website will be OWACW 2007.)

2   See *The Official Website of A Common Word, A Common Word 'White Paper' Booklet 2008*, The Royal AaL al-Bayt Institute for Islamic Thought, Jordan. *http://www.acommonword.com/index.php?lang=en&page=downloads* Any reference to it will be ACWWP 2009).

3   See Papal Address At University of Regensburg. "Three Stages in the Program of De-Hellenization", Libreria Editrice Vaticana, Zenit-The World Seen From Rome, September 12, 2006, accessed January 10, 2007. *http://www.zenit.org/article-16955?l=english*

4   See appendix A "An Open Letter and Call from Muslim Religious Leaders to" in Downloads and Translations A Common Word between Us and You, 2007. The Royal Aal al-Bayt Institute for Islamic Thought, Jordan accessed November 15, 2008. *http://www.acommonword.com/index.php?lang=en&page=downloads*

5   See appendix B "Loving God and Neighbor Together: A Christian Response to *A Common Word Between Us and You*" in *A Common Word 'White Paper' Booklet 2008*, The Royal Aal al-Bayt Institute for Islamic Thought, Jordan accessed November 15, 2008. *http://www.acommonword.com/index. php?lang=en&page=downloads*

6   See appendix C "The Final Declaration Issued at the Conclusion of the First Seminar of the Catholic-Muslim Forum, Rome 6 November 2008" in *A Common Word 'White Paper' Booklet 2008*, The Royal Aal al-Bayt Institute for Islamic Thought, Jordan accessed November 15, 2008. *http://www.acommonword.com/index.php?lang=en&page=downloads*

References

Abedin, S. Z. 1990. "Muslim Minority Communities in the World Today."
In *IslamoChristiana*. (16), 1-14.

Al-Bukhari, S. (n.d) "Hadith—Oneness, Uniqueness of Allah (Tawheed)."
9. Book 93. Accessed 25 February 2011. *http://www.esinislam.com/
Quran_And_Hadith/sahih_al_bukhari_hadith/sahih_al_bukhari_
hadith_book_93.htm*

Alfaisal, L. 2008. "The State of West-Islamic Dialogue." In *Islam and the West:
Annual Report on the State of Dialogue*, World Economic Forum, Geneva,
edited by Nancy Tranchet & Dinah Rienstra. Box 1.3. 16.

Al-Missned, M. B. N. 2008. "West-Islamic Dialogue: What It Is Really
About." In *Islam and the West: Annual Report on the State of Dialogue*,
World Economic Forum, Geneva, edited by Nancy Tranchet & Dinah
Rienstra. Box 3.4. 16.

Allport, G. W. 1942. *The Use of Personal Documents in Psychological Science*.
Social Science Research Council: New York.

Althusser, L. 1971. *Lenin and Philosophy and otherEssays*. New Left Books:
London.

Althusser, L. 1995. "Ideology and Ideological State Apparatuses (Notes
towards an investigation)." In *Critical Theory—A Reader*, edited by
Douglas Tallack, 298-313. New York: Harvest Wheatsheaf.

Arinze, F. 1997. "Christian-Muslim Relations in the Twenty-First Century." Talk Presented at Center for Muslim-Christian Understanding, History and International Affairs, Edmund A. Walsh School of Foreign Service, Georgetown University.

Armstrong, K. 2008. "The Meaning of Dialogue." In *Islam and the West: Annual Report on the State of Dialogue*, World Economic Forum, Geneva, edited by Nancy Tranchet & Dinah Rienstra. Box 1.2. 12.

Atkinson, J. M., and P. Drew 1979. *Order in Court: the Organisation of Verbal Interaction in Judicial Settings*. London: Macmillan.

Bakhtin, M. M. 2004. *Speech Genres and Other Late Essays*. Translated by vern W. McGee. Austin-Texas: Texas University Press.

Bawany, E. A. 1977. *Islam: theFirst and Final Religion*. Karachi: Begum Aisha Bawani Waqf.

Bhaskar, R. 1986. *Scietific Realism and Human Emancipation*. London: Verso.

Biber, D., S. Conrad. and G. Leech. 2002. *Longman Student Grammar of Spoken andWwritten English*. London: Longman.

Blommaert, J. 2005. *Discourse: Key Topics in Sociolinguistics*. Cambridge: Cambridge University Press.

Blumer, H. 1979. "Introduction to the Transaction Edition." In *Critiques of Research in the Social Sciences: An Appraisal of Thomas and Znaniecki's The Polish Peasant in Europe and America*. New Brunswick: Transaction Books.

Brown, G., and G. Yule. 1983. *Teaching the Spoken Language: an Approach Based on the Analysis of Conversational English*. Cambridge: Cambridge University Press.

Buaben, J. M. 1996. *Image of the Prophet Muhammad in the West—A Study of Muir, Margoliouth and Watt*. Leicester: Islamic Foundation.

Burman, E., and I. Parker. 1993. *Discourse Analytic Research: Repertoires and Readings of the Texts in Action*. London: Routledge.

Burr, V. 2003. *Social Constructionism*. London: Routledge.

Calder-Marshall, A. 1963. *The Innocent Eye: the Life of RJ, Flaherty*. London: W.H. Allen.

Cameron, D. 2000. *Good to Talk?* London: Sage.

Carter, R., A. Goddard. D. Reah. K. Sanger and M. Bowring. 2005. *Working with Texts:a Core Introduction to Language Analysis*, 2nd edition, Routledge, Taylor & Francis Group: London.

Carter, R., and M. McCarthy. 2006. *Cambridge Grammar of English*, Cambridge University Press: Cambridge.

Ceric, M. 2008. "Islam in Europe: Ideals and Realities." In *Islam and the West: Annual Report on the State of Dialogue*, World Economic Forum, Geneva, edited by Nancy Tranchet & Dinah Rienstra. Box 4.1. 45.

Chapman, C. 1998 *Islam and the West: Conflict, Co-existence or Conversion?* Cumbria-UK: Paternoster Press.

Chandler, D. 1994. *Semiotics for Beginners*. Wales: Aberystwyth.

Chouliaraki, L., and N. Fairclough. 2004. *Discourse in Late Modernity: Rethinking Critical Discourse Analysis*. Edinburgh: Edinburgh University Press.

Cooper, R. 1996. "Explanation and Simulation in Cognitive Science." In *Cognitive Science: An Introduction*, edited by D.W. Green, 23-52. Oxford: Blackwell.

Crafford, D. 1995. "Mission in a Multi-Religious Context." *Theological Forum* 23 (2).

Cragg, K. 1999. "Cross Meets Crescent: An Interview with Kenneth Cragg." In *The Christian Century*, February 17 1999, prepared by John C. Purdy for Religion online. Accessed 15 November 2009. *http://www.religion-online.org/showarticle.asp?title=500*

Curry, T., and A.C. Clarke. 1977. *Introducing Visual Sociology*, Kendall/Hunt: Dubuque. der Hoeven, M. J. A. 2008. "Respect." In *Islam and the West: Annual Report on the State of Dialogue*, World Economic Forum, Geneva, edited by Nancy Tranchet & Dinah Rienstra. Box 4.2. 47.

Derrida, J. 1976. *Of Grammatology*. Translated by Gayatri Chakravorty Spivak, Baltimore: The Johns Hopkins University Press.

Downing, A., and P. Locke. 2006. *English Grammar—A University Course*. Second edition. Routledge, Taylor Francis: London. New York.

Esposito, J. L. 2008. "A Dialogue for Results." In *Islam and the West: Annual Report on the State of Dialogue*, World Economic Forum, Geneva, edited by Nancy Tranchet & Dinah Rienstra. Box 1.4. 18.

Fairclough, N. 1992. *Discourse and Social Change*. Cambridge: Polity Press.

—. 1993. "Critical Discourse Analysis and the Marketization of Public Discourse." *Discourse and Society*. 4.

—. 1995a. *Critical Discourse Analysis: The Critical Study of Language*. England: Longman Education Group.

—. 1995b. "Ideology and Identity in Political Television." In *Critical Discourse Analysis*. Harlow: Longman.

—. and R. Wodak. 1997. "Critical Discourse Analysis." In *Discouse Studies: A Multidisciplinary Introduction*, edited by T. van Dijk, 258-284. 2. Sage: London.

—. 1999. "Democracy and the Public Sphere in Critical Research on Discourse." In *Challenges in a Changing World: Issues in Critical Discourse Analysis*, edited by R. Wodak. Vienna: Passagen Verlag.

—. 2000a. "Discourse, Social Theory and Social Research: the Case of Welfare Reform." *Journal of Sociolinguistics*. 4.

—. 2000b. *New Labour, New Language?* London: Routledge.

—. 2001. "The Discourse of New Labour: Critical Discourse Analysis." In *Discourse as Data—A Guide for Analysis*, edited by Margaret Wetherell, Stephen Taylor and Simeon J. Yates, 229-266. London: Sage Publications.

—. 2002. "Critical Discourse Analysis as a Method in Social Scientific Research." In *Methods of Critical Discourse Analysis*, edited by Michael Meyer and Ruth Wodak, 121-138. London: Sage Publications.

—. 2004. "Critical Discourse Analysis." In *Social Research Methods—A Reader*, edited by Clive Seale, 357-365. London: Routledge, Taylor & Francis Group.

FitzGerald, M. L. 2000. "Christian-Muslim Dialogue: A Survey of Recent Developments in the last 30 Years." Accessed 10 November 2009. *http://www.sedos.org/english/fitzgerald.htm*.

—. And J. Borelli. 2006. *Interfaith Dialogue: A Catholic View*. New York: Orbis Books.

Forgacs, D. ed. 1988. *A Gramsci Reader*. London: Lawrence and Wishart.

Foucault, M. 1979. *Discipline and Punish: the Birth of the Prison*. New York: Vintage Books.

—. 1982. "The Subject and Power." In *Michel Foucault: Beyond Structuralism and Hermeneutics*, translated by Hubert Dreyfus and Paul Rabinow. Chicago: University of Chicago Press.

—. 1990. *The History of Sexuality: An Introduction*. Translated by R. Hurley, 1. New York: Vintage Books.

—. 1995. "Truth and Power." In *Critical Theory—A Reader*, edited by Douglas Tallack, 66-77. New York: Harvest Wheatsheaf.

—. 2003. *Society Must Be Defended*. UK: PenguinBooks.

—. 2006a. *The Archaeology of Knowledge*. UL: Routledge.

—. 2006b. *The Order of Things*. UK: Routledge.

Garfinkel, H. 1967. *Studies in Ethnomethodology*. New Jersey: Prentice-Hall.

Gergen, K. 1996. "Social Psychology as Social Construction: The Emerging Vision." In *The Message of Social Psychology: Perspectives on Mind in Society*, edited by C. McGarty and A. Haslam. Oxford: Blackwell.

Gramsci, A. 1971. *Selections from Prison Notebooks*. London: Lawrence and Wishart.

Grodz, S. 2007. "Vie with Each Other in Good Works: What Can a Roman Catholic Missionary Order Learn from Entering into Closer Contact with Muslims?" In *Islam and Christian-Muslim Relations*, 205-218. 18 (2).

Habermas, J. 1971. *Knowledge and Human Interests*. Boston: Beacon Press.

—. 1989. *The Structural Transformation of the Public Sphere: an Inquiry into a Category of Bourgeosi Society*. Cambridge: MIT Press.

Haliday, M. A.K 1985. *An Introduction to Functional Grammar*. London. Australia: Edward Arnold Publisher.

Heim, S. M. 1995. *Salvations: Truth and Difference in Religion*. New York: Orbis Books.

Hick, J. 1989. *An Interpretation of Religion: Human Responses to the Transcendent*. New Haven: Yale University Press.

—. 1997. "The Possibility of Religious Pluralism: A Reply to Gavin D'Costa." *Religious Studies*. 161-166. 33.

—. 2000. "Religion, Violence and Global Conflict: A Christian Proposal." In *Global Dialogue: the New Universe of Faiths*, Centre for World Dialogue, Cyprus. 2. (1).

Ibrahim, A. 2008. "Islam and the West: The Myth of the Great Dichotomy." In *Islam and the West: Annual Report on the State of Dialogue*, World Economic Forum, Geneva, edited by Nancy Tranchet & Dinah Rienstra. Box 5.1. 58.

Janetzko, D. 2008. "Nonreactive Data Collection on the Internet." In *The Sage Handbook of Online Research Methods*, edited by Nigel Fielding, Raymond M. Lee and Grant Blank, 161-173. London: Sage Publications.

Kerr, D. 1989. "Muhammad Iqbal's Thoughts on Religion: Reflections in the Spirit of Christian-Muslim Dialogue." In *IslamoChristiana*, 25-55. (15).

Knitter, P. 1987. "Towards a Liberation Theology of Religions." In *The Myth of Christian Uniqueness*, edited by John Hick and Paul Knitter, 178-200. New York: Orbis Books.

—. 1995. *One Earth Many Religions: Multifaith Dialogue and Global Responsibility*. New York: Orbis Books.

Kritzeck, J. 1964. *Peter the Venerable and Islam*. Princeton: Princeton University Press.

Kochler, H. 1999. "Muslim-Christian Ties in Europe: Past, Present and Future." *IKIM Journal (Malaysia)*, January-June. 97-107. 7.(1).

Laclau, E. And C. Mouffe. 1985/1995. "From Hegemony and Socialist Strategy." In *Critical Theory—A Reader*, edited by Douglas Tallack, 340-353. New York: Harvest Wheatsheaf.

Leitch, V. B. 1983. *Deconstructive Criticism: an Advanced Introduction*. New York: Columbia University Press.

Maas, S., and J.A. Kuypers. 1974. *From Thirty to Seventy: a 40 Year Longitudinal Study of Adult Life Styles and Personality*. London: Jossey-Bass.

McAuliffe, J. D. 2008. "Context and Continuity is Crucial." In *Islam and the West: Annual Report on the State of Dialogue*, World Economic Forum, Geneva, edited by Nancy Tranchet & Dinah Rienstra. Box 5.2. 61.

McGarvey, K. 2009. Muslim and Christian Women in Dialogue—The Case of Northern Nigeria. Bern-Switzerland: Peter Lang.

Merton, R. K. 1967. *On Theoretical Sociology*. New York: Free Press.

Meyer, M. 2002a. "Between Theory, Method, and Politics: Positioning of the Approaches to CDA." In *Methods of Critical Discourse Analysis*, edited by Michael Meyer and Ruth Wodak, 14-33. London: Sage Publications.

—. and R. Wodak. eds. 2002b. *Methods of Critical Discourse Analysis*. London: Sage Publications.

Nasr, S. N. 2008. "We and You: Let Us Meet in God's Love." In First Catholic-Muslim Forum Conference, Vatican City, November 4-6. Accessed October 3, 2009. *http://acommonword.com/en/attachments/107_nasr-speech-to-pope.pdf*.

O'Halloran, K. 2003. *Critical Discourse Analysis and Language Cognition*. Edinburgh: Edinburgh university Press.

Panikkar, R. 1999. *The Intra-Religious Dialogue*. New Jersey: Paulist Press.

—. 2000. "Four Attitudes." In *Philosophy of Religion, Towards a Global Perspective*, edited by Gary E. Kessler, 532-536. New York: Wadsworth Publishing.

Pecheux, M. 1982. *Language, Semantics and Ideology*. London: Macmillan.

Peirce, S. C. 1931-58. *Collected Writings*, edited by Charles Hartshorne, 8. Cambridge, MA: Harvard University Press.

Phillips, N., and C. Hardy. 2002. *Discourse Analysis: Investigating Processes of Social Construction*. Thousand Oaks: Sage Publications.

Platinga, A. 1998. "A Defense of Religious Exclusivism." In *Philosophy of Religion: An Anthology*, edited by Louis Pojman, 517-530. New York: Wadsworth Publishing.

Potter, J. 1997. "Discourse Analysis as a Way of Analyzing Naturally Occurring Data." In *Qualitative Research: Theory, Method and Practice*, edited by D. Silverman, 144-160. London: Sage.

Potter, J., and M. Wetherell. 1987. *Discourse and Social Psychology: Beyond Attitudes and Behaviour*. London: Sage.

—. 2004. "Unfolding Discourse Analysis." In *Social Research Methods—A Reader*, edited by Clive Seale, 350-356. London: Routledge, Taylor & Francis Group.

Prior, L. 2003. *Using Documents in Social Research*. London: Sage Publications.

Quirk et al. 1985. *A Comprehensive Grammar of the English Language*. London. New York: Longman Group Ltd.

Rabinow, P. ed. 1984. *The Foucault Reader: An Introduction to Foucault's Thought*. London: Penguin Books.

Rahim, M. A. 2003. *Jesus, Prophet of Islam*. New York: Tahrike Tarsile Qur'an Inc., Elmhurst.

Reisigl, M., and R. Wodak. 2001. *Discourse and Discrimination: Rhetorics of Racism and Antisemitism*. London: Routledge.

Richardson, J. E. 2007. *Analysing newspaper: an Approach from Critical Discourse Analysis*. New York: Palgrave Macmillan.

Tranchet, N., and D. Rienstra. eds. 2008. *Islam and the West: Annual Report on the State of Dialogue*, World Economic Forum, Geneva.

Rowatt, W. C., L. M. Franklin. And M. Cotton. 2005. "Patterns and Personality Correlates of Implicit and Explicit Attitudes Toward Christians and Muslims." In *Journal for the Scientific Study of Religion*. 29-43. 44 (1).

Rosenthal, A. 1971. *The New Documentary in Action: A Casebook in Film Making*. Berkeley: University of California Press.

Sachs, D. 2008. "The Imperative of Integration." In *Islam and the West: Annual Report on the State of Dialogue*, World Economic Forum, Geneva, edited by Nancy Tranchet & Dinah Rienstra. Box 4.4. 50.

Sacks, H. 1992. *Lectures on Conversation*, edited by G. Jefferson, 2. Oxford: Basil Blackwell.

Said, E. W. 1979. *Orientalism*. New York: Vintage Books.

Saussure, F. 1983. *Course in General Linguistic*. Translated by Roy Harris. London: Duckworth.

Schegloff, E. A. 1972. "Sequenceing in Conversational Openings." In *Directions in Sociolinguistics: the Ethnography of Communication*, edited by J.J. Grumperz and D. Hymes. New York: Holt, Rinehart and Winston.

—. 1992. "Repair After Next Turn: The Last Structurally Provided Defense of Intersubjectivity in Conversation." In *American Journal of Sociology*, 1295-345. 97.

—. 1998. "Text and Context Paper." In *Discourse and Society*, 4-37. 3.

Schiffrin, D. 1994. *Approaches toDdiscourse*. Oxford: Blackwell.

Schwarz, H., and J. Jacobs. 1979. *Qualitative Sociology: A Method to the Madness*. London: Collier-Macmillan.

Scollon, R. 2002. "Action and Text: Towards an Integrated Understanding of the Place of Text in Social (Inter)action, Mediated Discourse Analysis and the Problem of Social Action." In *Methods of Critical Discourse Analysis*, edited by Michael Meyer & Ruth Wodak, 139-182. London: Sage Publications.

Sedgwick, P. 2001. *Descartes to Derrida: An Introduction to European Philosophy*. UK: Blackwell Publishing.

Simpson, P. 1993. *Language, Iideology and Point of View*. London: Routledge.

Sontag, S. 1978. *On Photography*. Harmondswoth: Penguin.

Swan, M. 2009. *Grammar*. Oxford: Oxford University Press.

Tajfel, H. 1982. "Social Psychology of Intergroups Relations." In *Annual Review of Psychology*, 1-39. 33.

Tallack, D. ed. 1995. *Critical Theory—A Reader*. New York: Harvest Wheatsheaf.

Taylor, C. 1992. *Multiculturalism and "The Politics of Recognition."* Princeton: Princeton university Press.

Taylor, S. 2001a. "Locating and Conducting Discourse Analytic Research." In *Discourse as Data—A Guide for Analysis*, edited by Margaret Wetherell, Stephen Taylor and Simeon J. Yates, 5-48. London: Sage Publications.

—. 2001b. "Evaluating and Applying Discourse Analytic Research." In *Discourse as Data—A Guide for Analysis*, edited by Margaret Wetherell, Stephen Taylor and Simeon J. Yates, 311-330. London: Sage Publications. ten Have, P. 1999. *Doing Conversation Analysis: A Practical Guide*. London: Sage.

Thomas, W. I., and F. Znaniecki. 1958. *The Polish Peasant in Europe and America*. New York: Dover Publications.

Van Dijk, T. A. 1983. *Strategies of Discourse Comprehension*. New York: Academic Press.

—. 1993. "Principles of Critical Discourse Analysis." In *Discourse and Society*, 249-283. 4.

—. 1997a. "The Study of Discourse." In *Discourse as Structure and Process—Discourse Studies, a Multidisciplinary Introduction*, edited by Teun A. van Dijk, 1-34. 1. London: Sage Publications.

—. 1997b. "Discourse as Interaction in Society." In *Discourse as Social Interaction*, a Multidisciplinary Introduction, edited by Teun A. van Dijk, 1-37. 2. London: Sage Publications.

—. 2001. "Critical Discourse Analysis." In *The Handbook of Discourse Analysis*, edited by D. Tannen, D. Schiffrin and H. Hamilton, 352-371. Oxford: Blackwell.

—. 2002. "Multidisciplinary CDA: a Plea for Diversity." In *Methods of Critical Discourse Analysis*, edited by Michael Meyer & Ruth Wodak, 95-120. London: Sage Publications.

Volf, M., G. Bin Muhammad and M. Yarrington. ed. 2010. *A Common Word: Muslims and Christians on Loving God and Neighbor*. Cambridge: Wm. B. Eerdmans Publishing Co.

Wagner, J. ed. 1979. *Images of Information: Still Photography in the Social Sciences*. Beverly: Sage.

Warren, M. E. 1995. "The Self in Discursive Democracy." In *The Cambridge Companion to Habermas*, edited by Stephen K. White, 167-200. Cambridge: Cambridge University Press.

Westerlund, D. 2003. "Ahmed Deedat's Theology of Religion: Apologetics Through Polemics." In *Journal of Religion in Africa*, 263-278. 33 (3).

Wetherell, M., and J. Potter. 1992. *Mapping the Language of Racism: Discourse and the Legitimation of Exploitation*. Hemel Hempstead: Harvester Wheatsheaf.

Wetherell, M., S. Taylor and S.J. Yates. 2001. *Discourse as Data: A Guide for Analysis*. The Open University. London: Sage Publications.

Widdowson, H. G. 1995. "Discourse Analysis: a Critical Review." In *Language and Literature*, 157-172. 4 (3).

—. 2004. "The Theory and Practice of Critical Discourse Analysis." In *Social Research Methods—A Reader*, edited by Clive Seale, 366-370. London: Routledge, Taylor & Francis Group.

Wodak, R., R. de Cillia. M. Reisigl and K. Liebhart. 1999. *The Discursive Construction of National Identity*. Edinburgh: Edinburgh University Press.

Wodak, R. 2002a. "The Discourse-Historical Approach." In *Methods of Critical Discourse Analysis*, edited by Michael Meyer and Ruth Wodak, 63-94. London: Sage Publications.

—. 2002b. "What CDA Is About—a Summary of Its History, Important Concepts and Its Developments." In *Methods of Critical Discourse Analysis*, edited by Michael Meyer and Ruth Wodak, 1-13. London: Sage Publications.

Wood, L. A., and R.O. Kroger. 2000. *Doing Discourse Analysis: Methods for Studying Action in Talk and Text*. Thousand Oaks: Sage Publications.

Yule, G. 1993. *The Study of Language: An Introduction*. Cambridge: Cambridge University Press.

Yusuf 'Ali, A. 2008., *The Meaning of the Holy Qur'an*. Maryland: Amana Publications

Zebiri, K. 1997. *Muslims and Christians: Face to Face*. Oxford: One World.

Zein, M. F. 2003. *Christianity, Islam and Orientalism*. London: Saqi Books.

Index

U

ummah consciousness, 2, 5-6

V

van Dijk, Teun, 14, 21-23, 32, 47, 154
Venerable, Peter, 52
  Liber Contra sectam sive haeresim
    Saracenorum, 52
  Summa totius haersis Saracenorum, 52
verbs
  modal, 42-43
  semimodal, 43

W

war on terror, 53, 83, 86, 89, 109
"West-Islamic Dialogue" (Al-Missned), 15
Wetherell, Margaret, 17, 148, 154
"White Paper," xiii-xvii, 17, 19, 33-34,
  36, 45, 50, 53-56, 60, 62, 93-97,
  99, 101, 107, 143
Widdowson, H. G., 24, 31
Wodak, R., 19, 22-23, 32

Y

Yule, G., 41

CPSIA information can be obtained
at www.ICGtesting.com
Printed in the USA
BVHW040337071122
651318BV00001B/5